SCOTLAND

SCOTLAND

INTRODUCTION BY ERIC LINKLATER

PHOTOGRAPHS BY EDWIN SMITH

NOTES ON THE PLATES BY OLIVE COOK

A STUDIO BOOK

THE VIKING PRESS · NEW YORK

Scotland
copyright page Viking Press edition

COPYRIGHT © 1968 THAMES AND HUDSON LTD

PUBLISHED IN 1968 BY THE VIKING PRESS, INC.

625 MADISON AVENUE, NEW YORK, N.Y. 10022

LIBRARY OF CONGRESS CATALOG CARD NUMBER: 68-19326

TEXT PRINTED IN SCOTLAND BY R & R CLARK, LTD., EDINBURGH

COLOR PLATES PRINTED IN GERMANY BY BOSS-DRUCK UND VERLAG KLEVE

PHOTOGRAVURE PLATES PRINTED IN FRANCE BY ETS BRAUN ET CIE MULHOUSE

BOUND IN SCOTLAND BY ANDERSONS EDINBURGH LTD DALKEITH

CONTENTS

TWELVE BLEAK MILES SOUTH of Hawick rise, in a brown irregular rectangle, the formidable walls of the castle of Hermitage. Behind it are moors and high pasture, tenanted only by sheep, silent but for the wind and the creak of peewits' wings and the thin chattering of wheatears; in front of it the increasing kindliness of Liddesdale opens a way into England, or England's western way into Scotland. It was to watch this way, and an enemy quartered in Carlisle, that the old castle was enlarged and rebuilt in the late 14th century and twice again within the next hundred years. Gaunt and desolate in its empty landscape, the great ruin is a memorial, not only to long ages of warfare, but, unexpectedly, to the perils and discipline that informed them. For the garrison of Hermitage there was an ample accommodation of privies, built indestructibly into its walls; and it may be inferred that the conditions of service were often or usually too dangerous to permit excursion into the open lands beyond its outer defences.

The earliest part of the castle has a history—or retains a legend—that is even older than politics and war. The great Norman family of de Soulis, sometime hereditary butlers of Scotland and lords of Liddesdale, once owned and held it; and William de Soulis, who flourished in the time of Robert the Bruce, was widely feared and long remembered as a wizard or warlock. In imitation of a Border ballad the exuberant Victorian poet Swinburne wrote a versified tale about him that begins:

> Lord Soulis is a keen wizard,
> A wizard mickle of lear:
> Who cometh in bond of Lord Soulis,
> Thereof he hath little cheer.

He has three braw castles to his hand,
*   That wizard mickle of age;*
The first of Estness, the last of Westness,
*   The middle of Hermitage.*

He has three fair mays into his hand,
*   The least is good to see;*
The first is Annet, the second is Janet,
*   The third is Marjorie.*

There is no historical foundation for Estness or Westness, nor other record of Annet, Janet, and Marjorie; but Swinburne reverts to tradition in his account of the death of Lord Soulis. So great was his evil power that he could defy even Death itself, were Death to come in any common aspect. Not until advice had been sought from that other wizard, the benign and excellent Thomas of Ercildoune—Thomas the Rhymer—was it possible to rid the Border of the wicked lord; but instructed by Thomas his executioners first bound him with a threefold rope of sifted sand, wrapped him in a cloak of lead, and boiled him in a brass pot poised above a bonfire in a nearby Stone Circle called the Nine Stone Rig. As Swinburne has it:

They boiled his body on the Ninestane Rig,
*   That wizard mickle of lear;*
They have sodden the bones of his body,
*   To be their better cheer.*

They buried his bones on the Ninestane Rig
*   But the flesh was a' clean gane;*
There was great joy in a' that border
*   That Lord Soulis was well slain.*

The Border between England and Scotland runs from the inner end of the Solway Firth, that is scoured by racing tides, to the town of Berwick-on-Tweed where the Tweed empties into the North Sea; and until the Union of the Crowns of England

I St Giles High Street, Edinburgh

The emphatic verticality of the Old Town as opposed to the classical horizontality of the New is well illustrated by these characteristically tall, rubble-walled tenement buildings dwarfing the small, brightly painted shops at ground level and the narrow passages leading into battered closes and courts. (*See also* pl. 2)

and Scotland in 1603 the Border was the scene of recurrent war, of habitual raiding and reiving. It was the breeding-ground of moss-troopers, of a predatory individualism, and the poetry of the Border ballads. The ballads range from legends of sorcery and magic, through the tale of Chevy Chase that moved the heart of Sir Philip Sidney (or so said Sir Philip) more than a trumpet, to the hard riding and harder arrogance of Johnny Armstrong and Kinmont Willie. At the far end lies the sinister magic of *Tam Lin*:

> *They shaped him in her arms twa*
> *But and a deer sae wild;*
> *But aye she grips and hauds him fast,*
> *The father o' her child.*

> *They shaped him in her arms twa*
> *A hot iron at the fire;*
> *But aye she grips and hauds him fast,*
> *To be her heart's desire.*

> *They shaped him in her arms at last*
> *A mother-naked man;*
> *She cast her mantle over him,*
> *And sae her love she wan.*

In the middle is the tale of Douglas and Percy at Chevy Chase:

> *The Percy leanèd on his brand*
> *And saw the Douglas dee;*
> *He took the deed man by the hand,*
> *And said 'Woe is me for thee!'*

II INVERARAY CASTLE, ARGYLLSHIRE. THE VICTORIAN BOUDOIR

The decoration of this room like that of the central, tower-like hall at Inveraray Castle dates from the mid-Victorian period, and no detail, not even the aspidistra in its green Minton pot has been changed. The extraordinary openwork chair of Indian calamander in the foreground, contrasting with the French bureau against the wall, is perhaps the most characteristic object in the room, but equally redolent of the period are the portraits of Campbell ladies in their heavy gilt frames, the two daguerreotypes on either side of the mantelpiece, the tall, snake-entwined opaque glass vases and the wallpaper by William Morris.

And at the nearer end there is the sad conclusion to the wicked life of Johnny Armstrong, betrayed (as was widely believed) by a device of King James VI:

> When Johnie cam' before the King,
>   Wi' a' his men sae brave to see,
> The King he movit his bonnet to him;
>   He ween'd he was King as well as he.
>
> 'May I find grace, my sovereign liege,
>   Grace for my loyal men and me?
> For my name it is Johnie Armstrang,
>   And a subject of yours, my liege,' said he.
>
> 'Away, away, thou traitor strang!
>   Out o' my sight soon mayst thou be!
> I grantit never a traitor's life,
>   And now I'll not begin wi' thee.'

From sea to sea the Border country heaves and descends in huge green billows of land, as if some gigantic ocean, broader by far and far more tempestuous than the Atlantic, had miraculously been stilled when all its enormous waves were smooth and solid, and all its valleys fluent and deep. This generous, more-than-oceanic landscape is nowadays dominated by small robustly peopled towns—Hawick, Selkirk, Melrose, Jedburgh, Galashiels—where fine tweeds are woven, woollen jerseys ingeniously knitted, and Rugby football is played with zest and true devotion. Modern life is lusty and broad-shouldered; but everywhere the past is still visible or audible. The ballads are not forgotten. Hermitage still dominates the road through Liddesdale. And a dozen or twenty miles on the other side of Hawick are the infinitely gracious, lamentable ruins of the abbeys of Jedburgh, Melrose, and Dryburgh.

Of Dryburgh by the river Tweed, in a noble park adorned by majestic trees, there is little left but some fine doorways that lead to vacancy, the barren shell of the north and south transepts of the abbey church. In 1140 the Augustinian White Canons of Alnwick in Northumberland made plans for a new extension of their order and began to build, as well as a great cruciform church, a splendid cloister and generous rooms for a community of canons, monks, and working brethren. Until the death of Alexander III and the War of Independence they spent their time, no doubt agreeably enough, in worship, litigation, the extension of their landed property, and work upon it. But when Edward I of England attempted the subjugation of Scotland, and Scotland objected to his policy, the Border abbeys were exposed to all the irrationalities of war, and Dryburgh was burnt in 1322. It was partially restored, and burnt again in 1385.

New building replaced what had been destroyed, but in 1544 there was another English invasion, and the abbey and the well-built, pretty town of Dryburgh were pillaged and burnt for the third time. From that conflagration the abbey never recovered.

The ruined abbey of Jedburgh has been embraced by a growing town, and the abbey church has retained enough of its original or restored structure to preserve, even now, a good deal of the dignity, splendour, and sense of total devotion with which men of the Middle Ages worshipped God their Maker. The red sandstone nave is magnificent, and in its boldness may exhibit the spiritual aspect of that hardy spirit which, down the ages, created other memorials in the Jeddart axe and Jeddart justice. The axe, a broad steel blade on a four-foot shaft, was the weapon preferred by the good people of the town when danger threatened; and according to Jeddart justice it was sometimes expedient to hang a man first and try him afterwards.

Under the three summits of the Eildon Hills are the beautiful and broken remains of Melrose Abbey. Within the Arthurian legend that wanders across Britain from Cornwall to the Firth of Forth, the Eildons are said to mark the grave of Uther Pendragon's son who married, for his unhappiness, the faithless beauty of Queen Guinivere; and Melrose has a history, more substantial than legend, but not less tragical. Like its neighbours, the abbey was founded in the 12th century, and originally covered a large area enclosed by a precinct wall more than a mile in length. In 1322 the monastery was sacked by Edward II, and some sixty years later Richard II destroyed what had been rebuilt. But it was built again, in great splendour and with ornamentation based on the Decorated and Early Perpendicular styles elaborated in the north of England; the Cistercians who founded the abbey had been men of simple habit, pledged to service and austerity, but their successors were familiar with grandeur and acquainted with pride. The church they built was sacked by the Earl of Hertford in 1545, but its ruins are massive—the cloister walk, the gable-end of the south transept, the great east window—and in a noble landscape they stand like the bones of a dead magnificence that Scotland could not defend.

He who did more than anyone to revive the old story of Scotland—to re-create it for the more tolerant world of the 19th century—was Sir Walter Scott, who, on the Tweed not far from Melrose, built the imposing house of Abbotsford, and when he died in 1832 was buried at Dryburgh. Literary fashions change, and nowadays Scott is not much read or highly esteemed; but his greatness is incontestable, his historical importance is very large, and Abbotsford is of fascinating interest. Scott was spendthrift and acquisitive too. He bought land with reckless extravagance, and made of his house a small museum to preserve and illustrate those artefacts and qualities of time past in which he took so much delight. A lock of Prince Charlie's hair, Rob Roy's gun, and a fine sword that belonged to James VI and was given to Montrose by Charles I—such things as these, and the broad river glinting beyond the dining-room windows—are clues to the mind and passions of a man whose ancestry was deeply rooted in the Border; in whom, perhaps, there survived something akin to the boldly acquisitive spirit of Kinmont Willie and Johnny Armstrong; but who, like the builders of the great abbeys, brought glory to the Border because his piety and genius were as deep and broad, as lively with imagination, as the creative spirit of the first Cistercians.

So much for Scotland's southern frontier. It is a small country, and its northern edge is only about two hundred and fifty miles from the inner corner of the Solway Firth. Its northern edge runs from Duncansby Head on the east to Cape Wrath on the west, and a straight line drawn between them would measure little more than seventy miles. For several hundred years the Border was subject to the recurrent danger of war with England, and since the last recession of the ice the northern edge has been torn and eroded, thrashed and belaboured by the turbulence of Atlantic gales and the Atlantic tide that rushes through the Pentland Firth into the shallower waters of the North Sea.

The Pentland Firth is so called because early geographers were misled by the pronunciation of local names they heard in Caithness and Orkney. When the Norsemen first came to Scottish shores, at some unrecorded date before the year 800, the islands and the northern parts of the mainland were largely, if not exclusively, inhabited by Picts; and what became the Pentland Firth was initially called the *Pettaland Fjordr*. In 1654 the Dutch firm of Blaeu published a map, drawn fifty years earlier, in which the firth is called 'Pichtland', but by 1700 it was modernised as Pentland because the native pronunciation was either 'Pechtland' or 'Pettland', and geographers from the south identified the strange northern name with the name of the Pentland Hills near Edinburgh.

To such ancient writers as Nennius and Gildas—shadowy figures of the 8th or 9th century—the Picts were a sort of proto-Vikings who had come from beyond the sea to make their first Britannic settlement in Shetland and Orkney; modern scholars, however, prefer to believe they were a Celtic people whose landfall was somewhere in the south, but whose subsequent progress was to the north. Their arguments, which are philological, are too complex to be unravelled here, but one can say with assurance that the Picts were solidly established in the northerly parts of Scotland, on the mainland and in the islands, before the Scots came from Ireland, in the 5th century, to settle in Argyll and the nearer western isles. Very little is known about the Picts, but they may not be dismissed as wandering barbarians devoid of manners and culture. They had their kings and courts, they were converted to Christianity by Columba, and they left, as relics of their hidden life, a multitude of incised stones whose symbols are sometimes marvellously naturalistic, more often stereotyped in forms that are elegant and sophisticated; and their society included mounted warriors and a priesthood.

About the middle of the 9th century Kenneth mac Alpine, king of the Scots, became also king of the Picts—probably as a reward, not only for military prowess, but for marrying an heiress—and by then there was in both Orkney and Caithness a Norse population of appreciable size: not Vikings, however, but peaceful settlers. The Vikings came later, and in their earldom of Orkney established a power that dominated the north until, towards the end of the 12th century, the earldom showed signs of its imminent decay.

Socially or ethnologically, then, the early history of the northern edge of Scotland is wholly different from that of its southern Border; and present appearances maintain he difference. In the extreme north-east lies the county of Caithness, much of it fairly flat and low-lying, with fine bold cliffs to mark its eastern shore, and some clearly glittering, sandy bays on the north. Much of the country is good agricultural land, it is almost treeless, and in early autumn, when the heather is in bloom, the upland moors wear a vestment of imperial splendour. The only town on the north coast is Thurso, on the salmon river to which the Norsemen gave the name of their god Thor, and to-day Thurso wears the flushed and prosperous look of recent expansion. The cause of its growth and increased wealth is a quite improbable monument to modern industry and applied science that sits on the shore a dozen miles to the westward. At Dounreay, in 1954, work was begun on an experimental nuclear power station, of the sort called fast breeder reactor, and beside the Pictland Firth, where a thousand years ago the Vikings trafficked, there is now balanced, among its attendant laboratories, a great sphere—the envelope of power—like a permanently anchored balloon; and the quiet little town of Thurso has put out new streets and acquired fresh interests for the accommodation of physicists and their families, technicians and accountants and engineers, and ever more children whose needs included new schools.

Westwards from Dounreay the road marches splendidly into nobler and more desolate country, whose desolation is made agreeable to the traveller by the contrast between shining beaches and the long bright firths that intrude from the north, and the immensity of empty landscape to the south, where majestic hills conceal the vacancy of a deserted land. A green selvage of population and the villages of Melvich, Bettyhill, Tongue and Durness confront the Pictland Firth. The long sea-lochs of Eriboll and the Kyle of Tongue invade the darkness of the hills with their pale bright colours. And beyond the Kyle of Durness there are six or seven miles of climbing moorland between the last village and the mainland's farthest lighthouse on Cape Wrath.

Before leaving the north a judicious traveller may feel inclined to visit, in Caithness, the scene of another industry, not much older than atomic power, but, unlike it, designed wholly for pleasure. Tourism is, perhaps, the modern world's most agreeable addition to life, and in several parts of the Highlands accommodation has lately been found for tourists whose primary demands are for shooting and fishing. The owners of sporting estates who find it impossible or impractical to maintain them for their private pleasure have, in some instances, turned a shooting-lodge into an hotel and opened moor and river to guests who will pay for the privilege. In Caithness, about fifteen miles due south of Dounreay, the lodge at Lochdhu and an hotel in the nearby village of Halkirk have become the tourist centres in an estate, of uncommon interest, that offers stalking, for stags in September and hinds in November; grouse shooting in August, and low-ground shooting in winter; falconry on the open moors; salmon fishing in the Thurso river, and trout fishing in a dozen hill lochs. Intelligent use, in this fashion, of land and water not otherwise profitable, may do much to bring life back to some empty and abandoned parts of the Highlands, and offer visitors—even visitors who neither shoot nor fish—the pleasure of living, for a little while, in country agreeable to the eye and distinguished by the fact that grouse and red deer and salmon still outnumber their human neighbours.

The road to Lochdhu winds thinly into the rolling vacancy of upland moors, with hills rising blue and abrupt beyond them. The last ten or twelve miles are a private road of a sort that reminds one of roads as they used to be: when I drove there, not long ago, I paused to watch a pair of grouse—red-wattled cock and hen demure—in the heather verge of the road; and half a mile farther on I had to stop until a lark, on the road in front of me, should finish its leisurely dust-bath. Curlew, crying with a pretence of melancholy, rose reluctantly and slowly flew away, and golden plover maintained a running conversation. In the dark heather the little hill lochs shone peacock-blue, and utter solitude in what appeared to be infinite space was the reward of walking in almost any direction.

Between Caithness and the Border—from the north shore of the Solway Firth about one-third of the way up a perpendicular drawn from it to the Pictland or Pentland Firth—Stirling Castle stands superbly on a dolerite crag above the river Forth. It may once have defended Lothian, the southern part of Scotland, from the Highland Picts, and the aptness of its familiar description as 'the key to the Highlands' is immediately apparent when, approaching it from the south, one sees beyond it, to the east the brooding heights of the Ochil Hills, and to the west the taller, darker menace of the hills of Menteith.

The town boasts some handsome buildings on the slope that rises from the south-east towards the rock of the Castle. Before the recognition of Edinburgh's supremacy, Stirling was virtually the capital of Scotland, its castle the royal residence. What is now the barracks was in its noble past James III's Parliament Hall; and James V, a monarch deeply interested in architecture, built beside it a palace in the Renaissance style. Some little way downhill from the Castle are the picturesque ruin known as Mar's Work, and the turreted building called Argyll's Lodging, architecturally the most important surviving town-house of its period: it was built in 1632, when civilisation was on the march and progress could be marked by the substitution—in rich men's houses—of cushioned chairs for wooden stools, of panelling for tapestry, and the introduction of tables as useful domestic furniture. But as well as lordly houses there are many lesser buildings to gratify the visitor, for in the 1930's an enlightened town council resolved to improve its older streets and preserve all the ancient houses that were worth preservation; and subsequent councils have realised, in the upper parts of the town, a policy designed for utility with dignity and dignity enhanced by the gaiety of discreet colour.

Beyond the meandering river the Wallace Monument rises tall above the Abbey Craig, and a little way down stream—but much disguised by the restless hands of time—is the field of Bannockburn where, in 1314, Robert the Bruce, with a small but highly trained army, defeated a vastly more numerous English host under Edward II. In 1964, on the site of his victory, a new monument to King Robert was unveiled by the Queen on the six hundred and fiftieth anniversary of the battle, and Robert's noble image, nobly mounted on a covered horse, seems to gaze inscrutably on the land he rescued from defeat. It is a land which he would now find quite unrecognisable. Here, in the waist of Scotland, is the Scotland that was so fiercely exploited in the Industrial Revolution. This is the part that brought riches to the country, and blackened its face in the process. Here, from central Ayrshire to Midlothian and parts of Fife, in something like one-tenth of Scotland's total area, live about three-quarters of the population.

The magnets that pulled the people in were the early development of cotton-spinning, linen-spinning, followed by weaving; and then the rich deposits of coal and iron-ore that became the grim foundations of heavy industry. The production of coal and pig-iron increased rapidly; steel-works multiplied; railways were built and quickly proliferated; the river Clyde was deepened to make a highway to the Atlantic. Ship-building became a fine art as well as a major industry, and in addition to creating with precision marine engines of remarkable efficiency, Scotland nurtured for their service a breed of engineers who found their vocation at sea. The Clyde was the mother of ships, and Glasgow grew larger and richer and much uglier. There were smaller industries in some variety, but not in a sufficient variety. The 'heavies' dominated the scene. The Industrial Revolution became conservative and lost imagination. It grew heavy in the stern, and immobile. About the field of Bannockburn, to mitigate its triumph, there are visible, for many miles on either side, the scars of social discomfiture and economic mishap.

But that admission is no confession of defeat. If Man is 'the glory, jest, and riddle of the world', it may be that Glasgow is the glory, jest, and riddle of our Caledonian parcel of the world. It grew too quickly for its own good, and when the houses of a prosperous bourgeoisie declined and darkened into slums, they defied demolition because they had been too well built. The people of Glasgow are notoriously hospitable, amiable, tolerant, yet enthusiastic. Their enthusiasms were at one time polarised on getting rich or getting drunk; at other times on achieving Grace and Salvation by piety or predestination; and are now more generally attached to one or other of the rival football teams, Rangers and Celtic. After a good many years of doubt and hesitancy, Glasgow seems about to defeat—has, indeed, begun to dislodge—the stagnation of heavy industry and the immobility of the slums. Its shape and appearance are changing month by month. Housing problems are being solved by vertical growth, and if the Clyde is no longer the universal mother of ships, its exuberant womb has taken to the discharge of other and lighter goods for the satisfaction of a world whose demands are also changing. In the last decade Glasgow seems to have been regaining a vitality that, for a generation or more, it appeared to have mislaid.

If it can recapture its former genius, then Edinburgh will have to seek again the spirit that saved it after Flodden threatened obliteration; after the Union of the Crowns presaged a bare, provincial future; after the Union of the Parliaments menaced the rump of Scotland's capital with immediate starvation and the ultimate collapse of utter redundancy. Against all the odds Edinburgh survived, and it may be that what Edinburgh needs to-day is the formidable challenge of the only city whose challenge it would take seriously.

In a small country local rivalries and antagonisms are intensified by proximity and the inescapable sight and sound of rival and antagonist; and to many of Scotland's

III BALNAGOWN CASTLE, ROSS AND CROMARTY.
THE SITTING ROOM.

This elegant Gothic room with its niched mantelpiece, slender clustered shafts, pointed panelling and ogival-headed doors and recesses was created as part of the alterations and additions begun in 1763 for the Laird of Balnagown, Sir John Lockhart Ross or Captain Ross as he was generally called. The decoration recalls that of Arbury, Warwickshire, and is typical of a fashion which appeared slightly later in Scotland than in the south.

inhabitants the debate of Westminster or the United Nations is dullish stuff in comparison with the constant liveliness of local dispute and gossip of the neighbourhood. Edinburgh is visibly a capital: handsome far beyond the average of cities, it stands dramatically astride the valley that divides the Gothic Old from the Classical New town. It has a history teeming with rough vicissitude, loud with anger, preaching, conviviality, and a ponderous wit; and all its history assures it of long life to come, if not of absolute immortality. Yet Edinburgh, like cities which have few of its advantages, is capable of an astonishing dullness of temper, indifference to appearance, and what seems to be a total lack of imagination.

In 1947, when all Britain was paying for its recent victory in a major war by the enforced practice of such austerities as, in the past, only defeated countries had to endure—its people lived on soya beans and offal, they could buy neither stockings nor petrol, occasional cream came from the black market rather than a cow, and sherry was an old man's memory—in those dark and dreary days Edinburgh defied the sad temper of the times by launching into a dull world, which received it with rapture, an International Festival of the Arts that asserted, against all contemporary evidence, the splendour of the human mind and the glory of its achievements. In that most dismal year Edinburgh, alone in Britain, proclaimed its belief that Britain, under Winston

IV MELROSE ABBEY, ROXBURGHSHIRE

The warm colour of the red sandstone upon which so much of the atmosphere of this ruined Cistercian Abbey depends is well conveyed in this photograph. The richness of the masonry shows little trace of the small, plain church that served the early needs of the austere community sent north from Rievaulx to found the Roxburgh monastery in 1136. The great window of the south transept with its curvilinear tracery and the canopied niches above it, once filled with sculpture, was the work in the 15th century of John Moreau or Morow, who was probably of French extraction. (*See also* pl. 49.) The part of the churchyard adjacent to the south transept, which forms the foreground of the photograph, contains a small tombstone inscribed in the mid Georgian period (1761) with a version of the powerful Middle English poem *Earth on Earth*:

> *The Earth goeth on the Earth*
> *Glistering like Gold,*
> *The Earth goeth to the Earth*
> *Sooner than it wold.*
> *The Earth builds on the Earth*
> *Castles and Towers,*
> *And Earth says to the Earth:*
> *All shall be Ours.*

Churchill, had won a victory which deserved recognition; and in 1947 Edinburgh devised and brought into being its most impressive celebration.

Since then the Festival appears to have become an institution. It has survived many difficulties, its success has prompted rival demonstrations in unexpected places, and for twenty years Edinburgh has seasonally been at home to living masters and the eternal masterpieces of the arts. But during that time Edinburgh has done nothing to provide new accommodation for orchestras and the ballet, for opera and drama, and experiment on the new circumferences that have opened outwards from the central traditions of music-making and the theatre. An act of creation has been succeeded by a somewhat bewildered acquiescence in what was done; and the apparent explanation is that Edinburgh's creative impulse was exhausted, perhaps for a generation, by the splendid parturition of its *annus mirabilis*.

The City Fathers deserve the greatest credit—more praise, indeed, than they have commonly been given—for the restoration and rehabilitation of many parts of the old town. Along the Royal Mile, that marches uphill from the palace of Holyroodhouse to the castle on its rock, there were aspects of dismal ruin that have been quite transformed; lively, elegant, or dignified shops and houses now stand where tumbledown squalor darkened the view. But in a period of time when there has been vast and ceaseless domestic building it is disappointing that Edinburgh has made no attempt to create a contemporary town in the spirit, and with the spacious vision, that inspired architects, City Fathers, and the citizens themselves to build so handsomely in the 18th and early 19th centuries. Bungalows beyond counting have covered near-by acres with the uniformity of their roofs and chimney-tops—with consternation the eye beholds flock after flock of them grazing on their tiny lawns—and all provide comfort, and the satisfaction of isolation within their own walls; but the new suburbs are shapeless and without form. They show no design.

In comparison with the men whose minds hatched a view dominated by Charlotte Square in the west, by St Andrew Square in the east—with the straight and broad and clean-faced channel of George Street running between them—the builders of Edinburgh's contemporary domesticity have been men of meagre imagination, or no imagination at all beyond the calculation of profit. Princes Street, that should be the handsomest boulevard in Britain—and is, indeed, on its unoccupied side—has progressively been demeaned and distorted by the replacement of older buildings with the flat-fronted, glazed ostentation of modern shops that have no architectural merit whatever, no architectural relevance to their situation.

There are many towns in England and Scotland where there might be little objection to the elimination of older building and its replacement by the vulgarity of occidental bazaars; but in Edinburgh, between natural grandeur and a considerable legacy of architectural dignity, there is so great an impaction of history that one feels it should all be revered and cherished and protected. But it isn't, of course, because people who live in a town can rarely afford to be sentimental about it. Sentiment has deadly enemies called rates and taxes.

Though Edinburgh has not seen fit to build a contemporary town, there are new towns rising from the roar and dust of concrete-mixers in the middle parts of Scotland, and a dozen miles south of Stirling—not quite so far from Bannockburn and the statue to Robert Bruce—is the urban novelty called Cumbernauld. Building was begun, or foundations were dug, in 1956, and ten years later the growing town was awarded an American prize for 'community architecture' against the competition of urban building from Finland to Brazil. To say, as has been said, that it is one of the architectural wonders of the modern world, is journalist's hyperbole, but Cumbernauld, on the edge of the Campsie Fells, offers to the approaching visitor an arresting view and then, on nearer inspection, a design of great ingenuity. Prominent on a ridge the many-tiered town-centre is surrounded by inhabited islets and broad working areas. Under one extensive roof are gathered shops and offices, places for entertainment and administration, a swimming pool, a skating rink, a supermarket and an hotel; a high school for sixteen hundred children is being built, and escalators, elevators, and gently sloping ramps convey shoppers and municipal officials, swimmers and housewives, schoolmasters and church-goers, from one level to another of the eight-storeyed, single-capped complex. Factories are already operating and emitting such varied products as articles made of glass fibre, carpets and underclothes, office equipment and window frames. A total population of 70,000 is envisaged, most of whom will probably come from Glasgow and its neighbourhood, and all of whom, according to need, will be adequately housed, taught, fed, cared for, and entertained. Cumbernauld is the creation of dextrous and imaginative minds, but its appearance does not suggest a capacity for endurance, a prospective longevity comparable, for example, with the castle of Hermitage.

Cumbernauld is not far from the line of the Antonine Wall that the Romans built, about the year 142, between the estuaries of the Clyde and the Forth. In England the Romans had established a rich and genial colony, destined to a longer life than most colonies enjoy; in the rougher geography of Scotland there was no such reward for conquerors as England had offered, but an aptitude for resistance to which rugged landscapes contributed as much as the fierce tribes who inhabited them. Scotland endured Roman punishment, but was never colonised. Hadrian's Wall, from the Solway to the Tyne, and the Antonine Wall across the waist of Scotland were both built as protection against the savage Caledonians, and except for an occasional foray beyond it and briefly occupied camps in Perthshire, the northern rampart marked the limit of Roman penetration. There is a common but erroneous belief that the line of the Antonine Wall neatly divides Scotland into Highlands and Lowlands. The truth, however, is more complicated.

Between the rolling hills of the Border and the narrow waist pinched by Forth and Clyde there lies a broad area, of varying aspect and differing character—some of it industrial, much of it good ploughland and pasture—that is indeed the richest, most populous, and important part of the Lowlands. But there are other Lowlands on the east coast, from Fife to the round shoulder of Aberdeenshire, and a narrowing strip from Kinnaird's Head, on the point of the shoulder, to Inverness at the innermost corner of the Moray Firth. North of Inverness are the farmlands of the Black Isle and Easter Ross, and beyond them the open landscape of Caithness: these are more truly Lowland than Highland, though Highland hills are their next-door neighbours.

Between the Firth of Forth and the broad estuary of the Tay the lands of Fife push out a blunt peninsula in which coal, golf, violent history, and patient scholarship are all domesticated. By the 16th century coal was beginning to acquire importance in the economy of Britain. So long as timber was plentiful and easily obtained, no one burnt coal in cottage or castle, for in open fireplaces its fumes were unpleasant. But as woods were cut and the timber-line receded, coal became necessary, and by the early years of the 17th century a landowner in Fife, Sir George Bruce of Culross, was mining coal from deep galleries—galleries below sea-level—that he had driven under the waters of the Firth of Forth. For three hundred years or more coal-mining was an expanding industry, for a long period manned by male, female, and juvenile labourers who were hardly better-off than slaves; and till recently the Fife coalfield produced more than 120,000 combustible tons a week. But coal is no longer the commodity that all industry uses, and on which all winter comfort depends; and it seems likely that golf will have a longer life. The Old Course at St Andrews will still be populous when the last pit is a viewless and deserted vacancy.

Three times in the 15th century a Scottish parliament forbade the playing of golf because idle men and youths preferred that useless game to practice at archery. On the field of battle English archers—who usually came from Wales—habitually defeated Scottish armies that went to war without adequate fire-power; yet indulgent Scots still played golf when they should have been shooting at the butts. About the middle of the 16th century, however, an archbishop of St Andrews affirmed his people's right of access to the sweet turf that now belongs to the Royal and Ancient, and when James VI came to the throne—he who was later James I of England—golf received the royal assent. James took his driver and sand-irons to London and, in 1608, under his patronage, the Blackheath club was founded. St Andrews may not be the birthplace of golf, nor the Royal and Ancient its oldest sodality, but golf was naturalised in Scotland at a very early date, and the sea-side links that march along its east coast are the most popular of luxuries and a national blessing.

It is an exaggeration to say that a powerful hitter can follow the coast and play all the way from North Berwick to Dornoch, but the exaggeration is not infinitely remote from the latitude of truth. From North Berwick to the championship course at Muir-field is no great distance, and a little way beyond Muirfield are the links of Gullane. Then come Aberlady and Longniddry, from where it would be a long drive to Musselburgh. On the Braid Hills a golfer might be embarrassed by the approaches to more than a dozen courses in the near neighbourhood of Edinburgh, but from Barnton the new road-bridge across the Forth might help him to reach Aberdour on the coast of Fife, and from there the way is open to Burntisland, Kinghorn, Kirkcaldy, Leven, and so across country to the four courses at St Andrews. He would leave Fife at Tayport, and aided by a hurricane might reach Barry or another championship course at Carnoustie in Angus. He would continue by way of Arbroath and Montrose to Stonehaven, and thence to half a dozen courses in or near Aberdeen; to Newburgh and Cruden Bay; to Peterhead, Fraserburgh, and so round the corner to Rosehearty and the links of Banffshire at Macduff, Banff, Cullen, and Buckie. Our golfer, still keeping to the coast, then enters Moray near Spey Bay, and by way of Garmouth approaches Lossiemouth, drives strongly towards Hopeman and Forres, and comes to a very agreeable course in the little shire of Nairn. From there he must cross the water to Fortrose in the Black Isle; there is more water between the Black Isle and Inver-gordon; and from Tain to Dornoch—a long chain of fairways beside the bright sands of the Dornoch Firth—a launching-pad rather than a tee would be needed, with a built-in propellent in the ball. There are, indeed, insuperable gaps throughout the whole course; but that is less remarkable than the fact that so much of it, from East Lothian to Sutherland, is playable.

The university of St Andrews, the oldest in Scotland, is probably older even than golf. It was founded in 1412, and sixty years later St Andrews was recognised by the Pope as the archiepiscopal and metropolitan see of Scotland. Before the Reformation the university had three colleges but only two faculties, arts and theology. Theologians have dictated some violent passages in the long history of St Andrews, and in 1546— fourteen years before the Reformation—the Protestant rebellion was heralded by a brace of murders. George Wishart was a Calvinist preacher and probably an English agent; the leader of the Catholic party in Scotland was Cardinal Beaton, Archbishop of St Andrews, a man of great power and equal brilliance. Wishart, who was some-times attended by a young man called John Knox—carrying, conspicuously, a two-handed sword—invited martyrdom by his provocative sermons, and the Cardinal, unwisely, responded. Wishart was arrested, tried and strangled, and his body was burnt. Three months later the Cardinal must have regretted his mistake.

Henry VIII of England and the English Privy Council approved a plan, concocted by the Cardinal's Protestant enemies in Scotland, to murder him; and early in the morning of the 29th May his assassins broke into the castle of St Andrews, seized the Cardinal in his bedroom, and hanged him from the castle wall. His assassins, numerously reinforced, held the castle for more than a year, but in 1547 it was reduced by the accurate bombardment of a French fleet. Among the prisoners taken was John Knox, whom his captors condemned to service as a galley-slave.

A hundred and thirty-two years later the long dispute between the Presbyterian and Episcopal forms of church government—or, more simply, between Kirk and King—was still unresolved, and neither side had much sympathy with the other. Episcopacy was restored, and stubborn Covenanters of the opposing faction were cruelly handled. Oppression bred new hatreds and nourished fresh thoughts of vengeance. James Sharp, for most of his life a Presbyterian, was offered preferment, and accepted. He became Archbishop of St Andrews and the object of intense ill will. But the Presbyterian zealots who, on the 3rd of May, 1679, were walking on Magus Moor, near St Andrews, were searching, not for him, but for the sheriff who was his friend and ally. It was by accident they encountered the Archbishop who, with his daughter, was being driven across the Moor in a carriage. Immediately—or so they claimed—they heard a call from God to put him to death, and halting his carriage they compelled him, by a threat to his daughter, to step out. They assured him that his days had now been numbered, they exhorted him to repent, they shot him, and cut him about the head with swords. Of his murderers only one was apprehended, and he had stood aloof from the deed of blood.

Nowadays St Andrews is the most agreeable of towns, and the handsome ruins which recall its past appear to fulfil their function without a trace of bitterness. A great tower, more than a hundred feet high, is the proud memorial to the early-12th-century church of St Rule, and the ruined castle where Beaton was murdered has so calm an aspect that it seems almost complacent. The cathedral was founded in 1160, and little remains of it except the east gable. There are walls and splendid gateways, deprived of any purpose, but beatifically reconciled to the loss of what stood above or behind them. A long stone pier points out to sea, past a little harbour, and every Sunday morning, during the University terms, the students in their short red gowns briskly perambulate to the far end, and return with a nice precision—red gowns going forth and red gowns coming home—while late arrivals still march seawards. In many places the ritual would seem pretentious and affected, but in St Andrews it is appropriate. It is surprising, indeed, that the students are so unaffected, so natural in their manner; for in such a place there must be temptation to pose and decorate the passing days with bright invention.

On the coast of Fife that faces south-east there are charming and sturdy villages— Crail, Anstruther, Pittenweem, St Monance—where that most benign of public bodies, the National Trust for Scotland, has done much to restore to its pristine strength and gaiety the vernacular architecture of the 17th century; and eighteen miles west and south of St Andrews is Falkland Palace, also restored though in a diminished shape. Here, in 1542, died James V, at the age of twenty-nine. He was able, active, cruel and oppressive to his rascally nobility, and much loved by his people. No one knows what caused his death, but after his army had been scandalously defeated at Solway Moss he may have drunk the poison of despair. He built, at Falkland, a *real* (or royal) tennis court, which happily has survived him.

Within a hundred and seventy years from the erection of St Andrews, three other universities were founded in Scotland: Glasgow in 1451, Aberdeen in 1495, Edinburgh in 1582. Glasgow languished, and for a good many years gave no promise of its subsequent vitality; but Aberdeen flourished under the fostering care of good Bishop Elphinstone. The papal bull, to authorise erection of a university, he solicited from pope Alexander VI, and taking Bologna as his model for what was soon to be called King's College, he persuaded the learned Hector Boece to become its first principal with a yearly salary of forty merks, or £2. 3s. 4d. sterling. Here, for the first time in Britain, provision was made for the teaching of medicine; but a hundred years after its foundation King's had grown a little old-fashioned. It resisted the new doctrines of the Reformation, and to remedy that sad state of affairs George Keith, fifth Earl Marischal and the richest nobleman in Scotland, founded a second university, called Marischal College, which was responsive to the more acceptable Presbyterian discipline.

Aberdeen is a city of remarkable character and striking appearance. It lies between two rivers, the Dee and the Don, and except for its new suburban periphery is clothed in sparkling adamant. It is a granite city, and on days when rain and sunshine alternate its walls reveal intrinsic jewels. It has industries, such as paper-making, but they are not obtrusive. Its granite quarries are less profitable than they used to be, because granite has become too expensive for its former functions. It has an extensive harbour, and its fleet of trawlers fish for haddock, cod, and profit as far from home as the well-guarded, off-shore seas of Iceland and the Faeroes. But intelligent visitors, while fully aware of the value of a fishing fleet, may still be puzzled to account for the obvious prosperity of a city quite unstained by smoke; and the good Aberdonians, trained to a sensible reticence, are unlikely to explain the mystery. The guess may be hazarded, however, that Aberdeen on the coast of a rich agricultural hinterland, still draws the income of a market town, as certainly it enjoys a countryman's health.

It has long been thought that parsimony is characteristic of Scotland as a whole, and of Aberdeen in particular; and history can explain the opinion and palliate the fact. In comparison with England, Scotland was a poor country, and from the days of James III till the 18th century its economy often suffered from an actual lack of money. No one can be prodigal with his purse when there are no coins in circulation, and recollection of such penury is no spur to extravagance even when better days refill the purse. But Aberdeen has a peculiar place in the legend of parsimony, for with a deliberate and defiant humour—with a stony enjoyment of its reputation for stinginess— it has invented and propagated a multitude of stories to prove and exemplify its ungenerous temper.

Some of them exhibit a taste for the macabre which owes much to memories of life as it used to be, when peril and poverty dominated life at sea, and hunger was no stranger on the cold uplands of Buchan. Such stories, for example, as that of the woman whose husband, a fisherman, was lost overboard. She mourned his death, and for several days her grief was aggravated because his body had not been recovered. Then, she was told, it had been found on the rocky coast by Slains, or Buchan Ness, or Rattray Head—some such stark and wintry landing—and she asked if she could see him. But no, she was told that would be unadvisable. For the partans had been at him. His body, when they found it, was 'fair covered wi' partans'. She wiped away her tears. She put aside disappointment, and recovered her composure. She remembered her hungry children. 'An' fit,' she asked, 'hiv ye deen wi' the partans?'—Or, in English, 'What have you done with the crabs?'

In the story of Aberdeen, however, there is no evidence of corporate or municipal parsimony. It is, on the contrary, a story of some gallantry and persistent enterprise; when, in or about the year 1800, the town began to grow into its modern shape along the bold and handsome line of Union Street, the cost of the street brought bankruptcy in its wake. But Aberdeen recovered and found, in Archibald Simpson, an architect who, after study in Rome, devised a proper style for shaping and handling his native

V CRICHTON CASTLE, MIDLOTHIAN

The may tree is in flower, but the light shines with a chilly glitter on dead branches, and the sloping expanse above Tyne Water, crowned by the castle ruins, recalls Keats's 'unmatured green valleys cold' and his 'aguish hills'. From this distance it is apparent how the original narrow, square medieval keep was enlarged by the addition of ranges of buildings inside the courtyard, among them the unusual Italianate wing, built in the 16th century to remind the owner, the fifth Earl of Bothwell, of his sojourn in Italy. (See also pl. 56)

granite. Much has been written, and deservedly so, in praise of Edinburgh's New Town and its builders; not enough in celebration of the new town of Aberdeen. Yet the Music Hall in Union Street, which Simpson built, is admirable in its simplicity, severity, and grace. He built Bon Accord Square and Bon Accord Crescent, which are delightful; for he was not overawed by granite, but in a crescent of houses could almost make that intractable stuff seem malleable.

The virtue of Union Street has lately been much obscured by modern addition, to which no commendation can be given; but the physical enlargement of Aberdeen elicits wonder and respect. As in Edinburgh, it is, in the main, a proliferation of bungalows that has pushed the city limits far into what was once its hinterland, and for its recent housing schemes land has been acquired with lordly extravagance. The population, still under 200,000, is a little larger than it used to be, but there has been no such increase as to tempt even the youngest of journalists to call it explosive. Yet

VI Carloway Broch, Lewis, Outer Hebrides

Broch is the Gaelic word for Dun, a fort, and the dry-stone monuments called brochs, which, though they have affinities with Iron Age forts in other parts of the British Isles, are unknown outside Scotland and are most numerous in the north of the country and the islands, are thought to have been the work of the Picts. They date from between 100 BC and about AD 400. Brochs are concentric in structure and rise to a height of 30 to 40 feet, with no windows in the outer wall. The inner wall is perpendicular, while the outer shows a bell-shaped curve. Set in the wall by the low entrance, some 4 feet high, is a guard chamber, and there are further chambers in the thickness of the walls, as well as a stair winding to the top of the broch, and galleries between the outer and inner walls. The Carloway Broch beside Loch Carloway, with distant views across the water to the hills of Uig and Gallan Head, is one of the most complete examples of this type of monu-ment to survive. Its stones are stained with a dull green patina which makes them one with the surrounding rocks.

VII Loch Culag, near Lochinver, Sutherland

This view across Loch Culag sums up the essentially noble character of this northernmost county of Scotland with its bare treeless expanses of moorland, its ancient rocks, thrusting up like relics of some tremendous spasm of the earth's crust, and its intense colour. The mountain in the background is Suilven, one of a group of grandly impressive peaks of Torridon sandstone. The heather in the foreground is Erica Tetralix, Cross-leaved Heath, Marsh Heather or French Heath, with rosy-red flowers and leaves arranged up the stems in groups of four.

the city now seems to occupy twice the area that lately was sufficient for its comfort, and its people are apparently more lavishly accommodated than any others in Scotland. No parsimonious finger has restricted town planning.

Of Aberdeen's two rivers, the Dee is more famous than the Don because its natural advantages—it flows through an open-hearted, gracious landscape—have been much enhanced by Royal favour since Queen Victoria, in 1848 or soon after, realised that her heart was in the Highlands and resolved to make a home for it at Balmoral. West of Balmoral, between upper Deeside and the valley of the Spey, the Cairngorms rise to an undulating and steeply divided plateau, over 4,000 feet high, of which the dominating peaks are Ben Macdhui, Braeriach, Cairn Toul, and Cairn Gorm. High on the slope of Braeriach are the Wells of Dee, the source of the river, and from there, through the Pools of Dee in the long and rocky pass called the Lairig Ghru, it flows under the Devil's Point and by the Forest of Mar to be constricted in a fine, boiling fury between the narrow granite walls of the Linn of Dee; having escaped from that confinement it runs more easily, but with great spirit, past Braemar and its old castle to Balmoral; and there, though the river does not pause, the traveller should. For south of the Dee rise the dark and tremendous cliffs, braided perhaps with snow, of Lochnagar; and none of the fine hills of Scotland—Cruachan or Schiehallion, Ben Lomond or Ben Nevis, or Liathach and Slioch in Wester Ross—wears more drama in its aspect than Lochnagar:

> *England! Thy beauties are tame and domestic*
> *To one who has roved o'er the mountains afar;*
> *Oh for the crags that are wild and majestic,*
> *The steep, frowning glories of dark Loch na Garr!*

So, in the enthusiasm of his youth, wrote the poet Byron; of whom more presently.

From Balmoral to its mouth at Aberdeen the Dee flows eastward for some forty miles, through the pleasant villages of Ballater, Aboyne, and Banchory; and near the last is one of a pair of small and lovely castles: Crathes, east of Banchory on the Dee, and a dozen miles to the north-west Craigievar, south of Alford on the Don. There are castles by the score in Scotland, most of them in ruins, but none more charming or more elegant than these, of which the former was built by 1600, the latter (a little younger) by 1624. The severity of their straight high walls is mitigated by the gaiety of their turrets and painted ceilings, and baronialism, one feels, has made a happy marriage with domesticity.

The Don is less stylish than the Dee, its waters do not flash so brightly; but none should lightly depreciate it, for its votaries are ardent. There is an old rhyme which claims:

32

> *A mile o' Don's worth twa o' Dee,*
> *Except for salmon, stone, and tree.*

And another which recalls the danger of sudden floods, to which the Dee notoriously is subject:

> *Bluidthirsty Dee*
> *Each year taks three,*
> *But bonny Don*
> *Asks for none.*

From Cock Bridge and Corgarff the Don runs usefully down to water the rich farm-lands of Aberdeenshire. It is a workaday river, with papermills near its mouth. But the Don and some of its tributaries are good trout streams, and there are those who say it runs to a music of its own, unlike that of any other river. Near its mouth, where it is black and deep, it is dignified by the Auld Brig o' Don, or the Bridge of Balgownie, which is thought to have been built by Henry Cheyne, Bishop of Aberdeen in the days of Robert the Bruce.

Now Byron must be admitted to the scene again; for suddenly, in the tenth canto of *Don Juan*, he remembered the Scotland of his youth—his running pen scribbled *Auld Lang Syne*—and for a moment he yields to sentiment:

> *But I am half a Scot by birth, and bred*
> *A whole one, and my heart flies to my head,—*
> *As 'Auld Lang Syne' brings Scotland, one and all,*
>   *Scotch plaids, Scotch snoods, the blue hills, and clear streams,*
> *The Dee, the Don, Balgounie's brig's black wall,*
>   *All my boy feelings, all my gentler dreams*
> *Of what I then dreamt. . . .*

As a boy he attended for some years the ancient Grammar School of Aberdeen, and his half of Scottish blood—more potent by far than his English moiety—he fetched from one of the most powerful and turbulent of Scottish families. His mother was a Gordon of Gight, and the chief of the Gordons was called 'Cock o' the North'. To the daring and *panache* of the Highlander they added the wealth and resolution bred on their Lowland estates, and after they had complicated history for three or four hundred years it was typical of the family that the fourth Duke of Gordon, in 1794, should raise a battalion of Gordon Highlanders with the aid of six pipers and a Duchess so lovely that when she promised a kiss for every recruit, recruits came in from every parish of the north-east.

*

The northern part of Scotland—the larger part beyond the waist—is diagonally divided by the Great Glen and a continuous waterway running from Loch Linnhe in the south-west to the Moray Firth in the north-east. The waterway consists of three narrow lochs, Lochy, Oich, and Ness, which are linked by the several segments of the Caledonian Canal. At the south-west entrance there are vast, romantic landscapes, desolate and splendid, and tall islands beyond the dividing sea. The north-eastern mouth opens on quite a different scene. There are three deeply intrusive firths—the Beauly, Cromarty, and Dornoch Firths—but the lands they enclose are fertile, prosperous, and gentle of aspect. Of the small towns or villages in this area, Cromarty on the Black Isle deserves attention because it has some uncommonly good houses, and two of its native sons became widely known for their remarkable achievements. As men they were utterly and strikingly different, and their achievements were quite unrelated. But each of them was manifestly Scotch in his own exaggeration of Scottishness.

The older was Thomas Urquhart, scion of an ancient family, born in 1611, and educated at King's College, Aberdeen. He travelled on the continent, and in 1641 was knighted by the royal hand of Charles I at Whitehall. A dandy and an ardent Royalist, he fought at the skirmish called the Trot of Turriff, and again at the battle of Worcester, where he was wounded and made prisoner. By Cromwell's order he was released in 1651, and according to tradition died of a fit of laughter on hearing of the restoration of Charles II.

His title to fame and continuing favour derives from his translation of Rabelais, and there is general agreement that of the several gifted translators in the most richly fruitful century of English literature, Sir Thomas was the greatest as well as the last. Such was his genius that he out-matched the riotous fecundity of Rabelais's own prolific mind, and where Rabelais's French flows full as the Wye when spring rains have fed it, Urquhart's English may run with the Rhone's deep-roaring flood. In the summer warmth of his mind he hatched new words and sent them out in flocks like homing pigeons; but of constant temperature was his sense of honour. Nowhere does his own voice more clearly sound than in his description of the abbey of Thélème and its inmates, whose motto was *Fay ce que vouldras*:

'In all their rule, and strictest tie of their order, there was but this one clause to be observed, DO WHAT THOU WILT.

Because men that are free, well-borne, well-bred, and conversant in honest companies, have naturally an instinct and spurre that prompteth them unto vertuous actions, and withdraws them from vice, which is called honour.'

Heads have been shaken with heavy disapproval over the elaborate nonsensicalities that Urquhart wrote about mathematics and his own genealogy: with an appearance of infinite labour and exactitude he traced his descent from Adam. No one, however, has suggested that these exquisitely absurd lucubrations are examples of Scottish humour at its worst: a ponderous and pedantic humour, that only an aberrant scholarship could father, and only the most indulgent toleration of its own jokes would license. Much of Urquhart's elaborate pedantry is, almost certainly, jocularity in a heavy disguise, and should, perhaps, be compared with *Finnegan's Wake*. Both he and Joyce wore their monstrous erudition as if it were the top-heavy finery of a Highland drum-major.

Cromarty's other distinguished son was Hugh Miller, a man of humble birth who by the exercise of his own intellect and determination became a scholar, a man of letters, and a person of considerable influence in the affairs of his own time. Born in 1802, he was left an orphan at the age of five when his father, a sailor, was drowned at sea. But he was not left destitute. With the help of two kindly uncles he got what education was available, and might have gone to college had he not decided that what he wanted to be was a stone-mason; and in the circumstances of the time he served his apprenticeship in a quarry. He had, it seems, discovered a precocious interest in geology, and in that more leisurely age masons and quarrymen appear to have admitted that outdoor work in the winter months was uncongenial; so they stayed at home. Young Miller had time for study, and by some means or other he got access to books.

He worked in Edinburgh and Inverness, and at an early age published *Poems by a Journeyman Mason*. They were not good poems, but they won for him favour, patrons, and opportunity. He became a journalist, and then, very curiously, a banker. He married an attractive young woman of a social class superior to his own, and in the intervals of banking wrote and published his *Scenes and Legends of the North of Scotland*. Then he intervened in that great ecclesiastical dispute of the mid-century which led to the Disruption—or great schism of the Presbyterian church—and was promptly offered the editorship of a newspaper called the *Witness*, which argued the case for what became, in opposition to the 'Auld Kirk', the 'Free Kirk'. But Miller, as editor of the *Witness*, showed not only his piety and knowledge of church history, but the singular independence of his mind and his passionate interest in rocks. In his editorial columns he criticised current literature and works of science, and wrote those essays on the Old Red Sandstone which brought him his contemporary fame. He had found fossils in a geological formation which, until then, was thought to be devoid of fossils.

With his scientific aptitudes and scholarship he combined the simple faith of a somewhat earlier time, and in his *Footprints of the Creator* he rejected the evolutionary theory while describing with grace and particularity his discovery, in the Red Sandstone of Orkney, of a primitive fish-like creature called Asterolepis, or, more resoundingly, *Pterichthys Milleri*. For general reading, however, his most attractive work is *My Schools and Schoolmasters*, which in a series of vivid pictures includes, somewhat unexpectedly, an account of the yearly cock-fights at the grammar school of Cromarty. He wrote with vigour and fluency, he had the gift of lively description, and his pages bear the imprint of a hearty and most likeable personality. But at the age of fifty-four he killed himself.

In the 19th century the self-taught man, of letters or science, was a recognised and perhaps easily recognisable feature of the social life of Scotland; and all too often he died untimely because the exertions of his early years had over-taxed a strength insufficiently nourished by the sack of oatmeal which, for his sustenance in a university term, he had brought from a croft in Argyll or Wester Ross. A talented boy—'a lad of parts', as he was called—was usually given help or patronage to carry him to the university, but all too seldom enough money for proper food and clothing. He nourished his mind and independence, but his health declined. Hugh Miller is typical of a class, but outshines his class because his talents were so manifestly superior, and because his writing reveals a man who was intrinsically good—intensely serious without being pompous—and lovable without ever employing tricks to elicit favour.

In Cromarty, that engaging little town which looks northward across a narrow, tidal firth, his white-harled cottage is immaculately preserved by goodwill of the National Trust; and in the parish church, not far away, there is a plaque to the memory of Sir Thomas Urquhart. They both deserve obeisance.

The Atlantic coast presents Scotland in its most obviously attractive and romantic aspect. From Cape Wrath to Ardnamurchan is, perhaps, a hundred and fifty miles, and most of it is pierced by sea-lochs and overlooked, from the landward side, by the high hills whose names read like the leaders of a great host of Gaelic chivalry: Foinaven, Ben Stack, Quinag, and Canisp; Ben More of Coigach, An Teallach, and Slioch; Liathach and Ben Bhan. Their names resound, and the scenery carries echoes of their splendour. But the Gaelic charm—the almost excessive charm—of that sea-loud coast is that within majestic vistas or under frowning heights there are small, idyllic glens, bright with broom and little white roses in their season, and lochans which bear an islet aflame with rhododendrons that reflect their colour in still, dark water. Vast, savage heights and harebells, tormentil, in their shadow; the Atlantic thundering on bright beaches, and ring-plover, tiny dunlins, stepping daintily among the stones—there's the stereotype of West Highland scenery: an enchanting collaboration of all that's biggest and boldest with much that's small and delicate, ephemeral yet blessedly recurrent.

Within the last ten or a dozen years the roads to the west have been greatly improved, though they are still quite different from the broad and arid highways that dissect so much of the modern world. Better roads have brought an increasing number of visitors into the handsome vacancy of the long coast-line from Argyll to Sutherland, and a major attraction has been the wholly unpredictable luxury of the great garden at Inverewe. About a hundred years ago, a young man called Osgood Mackenzie acquired a large sporting estate, and having built a house on a small, exposed, and barren peninsula in Loch Ewe—between Gairloch and Gruinard Bay—he resolved to plant that unpromising ground and make a garden. On a bed of peat and Torridon red sandstone he persuaded Austrian and Scots firs and a few hardwoods to grow, and within their shelter added copper beech, horse chestnuts, bird-cherries, spruce, and scarlet oak; and after them he introduced such improbable exotics as eucalyptus, arbutus, tree rhododendrons, and bamboos. The windswept, bare peninsula is now a little forest, ablaze with colour in the spring and early summer, for in the warmth of the Gulf Stream camellias and magnolias flourish, with natives of Chile and Australia, Kaffir lilies and the giant forget-me-not of the Chatham Islands, palms and hydrangeas. There is a lordly kitchen-garden, raised above an old sea beach, and on either side the shores of the loch reach out into the Atlantic as bare and dark and rocky as was the garden ground before Osgood Mackenzie decided to essay the manifestly impossible, and, within his own lifetime, brilliantly succeeded.

He also wrote a book of great fascination, *A Hundred Years in the Highlands*, in which he recorded the astonishing richness of wild life in Wester Ross, and what he did to exterminate it. Ospreys and golden eagles and whooper swans all fell victim to his expert gun, or his hobby of egg-collecting—grouse and snipe and black-game were killed by the thousand—otters, badgers, wild cats, pine-marten, roe and red deer were slaughtered with enthusiasm—many a miraculous draught of fishes was hauled ashore—and towards the end of his long life the venerable Mackenzie, bearded like Santa Claus, patriarchal and benign, looks about him in sad perplexity because there is nothing left to shoot or catch. 'What a big pile it would make', he writes, 'if all the black-game I shot there between 1855 and 1900 were gathered into one heap. Now, alas! there are none, and why, who can tell?'—But he made a garden of incomparable charm, which to innumerable people gives rare and unexpected pleasure.

South of Poolewe the Applecross peninsula looks over the sea to Raasay and the Isle of Skye. From the head of Loch Kishorn the road climbs in a spectacular zigzag to the *Bealach nam Bo*, the Pass of the Cattle, an ascent of more than 2,000 feet in less than six miles, and from the other side of that bare and stony height one looks down at a lush green parkland on the Atlantic shore.

Between Skye and the mainland the sea runs narrowly through Kyle Rhea and the Sound of Sleat, and beyond the brisk and lively fishing port of Mallaig are the white sands of Morar and Arisaig. Parts of Loch Morar are more than a thousand feet deep, which equals the oscillating lake of Geneva. The sands are not as white as snow, but against an emerald sea their pallor is remarkable, and on a fine day in early summer the brilliance of the scene can astonish even those who think themselves prepared for it. Except in its middle parts, most of Highland Scotland is a many-coloured country, but in no corner of it is there a brighter, more genial, or more various splendour.

In fairness, however, to another part of the country it must be admitted that a good many artists—painters, that is, *croyants et pratiquants*—have shown their preference for some little towns on the much indented south coast of Galloway. The province of Galloway comprises the two shires of Wigtown and Kirkcudbright, which for a dark reason is pronounced Kirkoo'bry, and many include (though this will be disputed) those parts of Ayrshire south of the county town. Before roads and the internal combustion engine demolished geography's natural barriers, it was thought to be remote, and its history reflected its relative isolation. Its moors and forests were too difficult for the Romans, but for long years it was open to the Norsemen—Vikings, traders, or settlers—who had established themselves in the nearer parts of Ireland. The old lords of Galloway asserted their independence, and for a century or more, from the mid 14th to half-way through the 15th, the arrogant and lordly house of Douglas was a recurrent menace or limitation to the power of the throne. According to tradition the first Christian missionary to Scotland was St Ninian, whose *Candida Casa*, said to have been built in 397, may have stood near the ruined chapel at Isle of Whithorn in the extreme south of the bleak peninsula called The Machers; and in the 17th century the people of these parts were Covenanters of the most rabid sort: they became the far left wing of the Presbyterian Reformation.

VIII EILEAN DONAN CASTLE, ROSS AND CROMARTY

The castle of the MacKenzies, originally built in the 13th century, stands on a tiny island, approached by a narrow causeway, where three sea lochs meet—Loch Duich, Loch Long and Loch Alsh. It is a tower house of the standard pattern with a courtyard and traditional features such as corbelled angle turrets, stepped gables and a staircase turret. But the present fabric is very largely a reconstruction of 1932, carried out by Col. Gilstrap MacRae, for the castle was severely damaged in the Battle of Glen Shiel in 1719. Three hundred Spanish soldiers had landed in the Glen and had been joined by the MacRaes and MacKenzies, but the incipient rising was crushed by troops from Inveraray, before it had got under way. English frigates sailed into Loch Duich and Eilean Donan was bombarded from H.M.S. Worcester. Viewed from a little distance in its unaltered setting of tumbled mountain, loch and sea, surely one of the most picturesque sites in Britain, the restored castle looks much as its medieval occupants saw it.

In Wigtown, near the head of Wigtown Bay, there is a stone in the churchyard which pretends to commemorate the martyrdom of two women, Margaret McLauchlan and Margaret Wilson, ardent Covenanters who are said to have been tied to stakes, and left to drown in tidal waters, near the mouth of the river Bladnoch. There are those, however, who see in the memorial merely an early example of political propaganda, and declare that both women were known to be alive long after their reputed death in 1685. A few miles above the bay, on the river Cree, the small town of Newton Stewart lies in a lush, pastoral landscape and offers a distant view, to the north, of the hills about Loch Trool. There, in 1307, Robert the Bruce won a small but important victory over the English: important because it came after a period when hope must have been vanishing like the last of the old moon behind a cloud; and then, like a rainy sunrise, hope shone faintly again in a new sky. The Galloway hills rise to heights of 2,500 feet and more, but their contours give no great impression of height.

IX COMRIE, PERTHSHIRE

The graceful whitewashed church on the banks of the Earn with its pretty castellated tower and Gothic windows was built by John Stewart in 1805. The plain oblong plan with a tower at the west end conforms to the type of kirk which was most popular throughout the 18th and early 19th centuries.

The exquisitely tranquil atmosphere of the photograph does not entirely correspond to the character of Comrie. The church now serves the parish, not as a place of worship but as the headquarters of a youth club, the 'Flambeaux', and the building stands immediately above the great geological flaw separating the Highlands from the Lowlands, so that it is frequently shaken by minor earth tremors.

X TRAQUAIR HOUSE, PEEBLESSHIRE

Traquair, built as a royal hunting lodge, is one of the oldest houses in Scotland. The original tower house is incorporated in the northern end of the present building, which dates from the 16th and 17th centuries. The angle and staircase turrets of the latest extension, jutting forward from the rest of the building, as well as the square turret belonging to the oldest part of Traquair, show an unusual type of corbelling, a stone version of the jettying of half-timbered houses. The walls are harled and washed a silvery grey colour, reflecting the clear light and contrasting with the vivid green of the setting. The forecourt and service wings were laid out between 1695 and 1705 for Charles, fourth Earl of Traquair, by James Smith, a master mason who had worked with Sir William Bruce on the remodelling of Holyrood House (see pl. 10). Smith was also responsible for the wrought iron screen and stone piers surmounted by the classical, sculptured urns which so strangely confront the traditional façade of the tall house.

Kirkcudbright on the Dee, at the head of Kirkcudbright Bay, is blessed by the tide and suffers from its recession. The tide ebbs to a prodigious distance and exposes a vast expanse of mud which is profitable for wading birds and may prettily reflect the light of a changing sky; but there is too much of it, and often the tide seems reluctant to return. But when it does, Kirkcudbright with its brightly coloured houses and its fine old tolbooth is marvellously situated in the midst of waters that play the looking-glass for marching clouds above.

Some twenty miles to the east, and due south of Dumfries, are the village and parish of Kirkbean, where he who is generally known as Paul Jones—and who lived to be acclaimed as the first hero of the American navy—was born in July 1747. He was the reputed son of John Paul, gardener to Robert Craik of Arbigland, a member of Parliament; but John Paul had married Jean Macduff, a Highland girl who had been cook at Arbigland; and in local opinion the boy's father was not the gardener, but his employer. He was a boy of remarkable ability, and taking to the sea at an early age, served as mate aboard a slaver, and at twenty-one was apparently given command of a merchantman. Then he retired to live in America, where an older brother had settled in Virginia, and in 1775, when war broke out between England and her rebellious colonies, he offered his services to the rebels and immediately found employment.

After some useful service on the American coast he was promoted, and sailed to France in command of the sloop-of-war *Ranger*. From Brest he turned north, and at Whitehaven, on the English side of the Solway Firth, surprised the garrisons and spiked the guns in the two forts that guarded the harbour. A few days later he defeated and captured the British sloop-of-war *Drake*, and took her to France. Again promoted, he sailed in command of a squadron of seven ships, most of which deserted him. A sudden gale frustrated his attempted attack on Leith, but off Flamborough Head his squadron, by then reduced to two ships, *Bonhomme Richard* and *Pallas*, engaged the British ships *Serapis* and *Countess of Scarborough*, and after a desperate battle of three or four hours, Paul Jones emerged the victor. He transferred his flag to *Serapis* shortly before his own deeply wounded *Bonhomme Richard* sank.

That concluded his active service, except for an unsatisfactory year of employment as a Russian rear-admiral under the Empress Catherine. Four years later, in 1792, he died in Paris, and in 1905 an American fleet escorted his body—well preserved in a lead coffin—across the Atlantic to the naval academy at Annapolis, where it was re-interred with conspicuous pomp and elaborate ceremony. Jones is said to have left among his papers 'a copious memoir of his life written with his own hand'; but if that is true, the memoir has regrettably disappeared. One would like to know a little more about his motives. His service under the Russian empress seems to exclude or deny such a pure and burning love of liberty as otherwise might well have been the reason for his immediate offer to fight for the indignant colonies, and for his valiant and resolute efforts on their behalf. He changed his name from John Paul to Paul Jones, and that does suggest a resentment, long suppressed but eventually explicit, against the poor gardener who had, presumably, been bribed to marry the girl whom his master had put in the family way. Darker and deeper may have been his hatred of the father who disowned him—Mr Craik the laird of Arbigland, and a member of Parliament— and indistinguishable from it, perhaps, was his hatred of the class and country that Craik represented. Paul Jones, father of the American navy, did not choose to live out his life in the land of his adoption, but preferred France; and one has to accept the possibility that hatred of his enemies was stronger than love of his friends. Mr Craik may have had much to answer for.

Between fifty and sixty miles north-west of Kirkbean, and within the confines of Galloway if it be accepted that Galloway includes much of Ayrshire, is the birthplace of a greater man whose life, and the motives that seem to have determined it, have excited more controversy than Paul Jones ever roused, and whose nature was certainly more complex and infinitely richer. Alloway is a couple of miles south of Ayr, and its sole distinction—but that is enough—is that there, on the 25th of January, 1759, a child was born to another gardener, William Burns (or Burnes) and Agnes his wife, who was christened Robert and lived to become, not only a poet of classical accomplishment who wrote in a fine literary form of the Lowland Scots vernacular, but a man who bequeathed a cult, immensely popular, not wholly insincere, and emerged as a folk-hero who, like a golden sovereign or a common penny, bore different designs on his reverse and obverse sides.

Robert Burns, and some of his verses, are related by animosity to the extravagant left-wing enthusiasm of those Covenanters of the south-west whose successors, in his time, were parish ministers and elders of the sort he satirised in *Holy Willie's Prayer*— elders who praised a God made in their own image—

> *O Thou, that in the heavens does dwell,*
> *Wha, as it pleases best Thysel',*
> *Sends ane to heaven an' ten to hell,*
> *A' for thy glory,*
> *And no for onie guid or ill*
> *They've done afore Thee!*

Robert Burns, in whom nature opposed restraint and whose behaviour was sometimes indiscreet, had been sorely drubbed by the presbyters of his parish, and in revenge derided the very origin, the Calvinistic foundation, of the authority they claimed. He went farther than that. In *The Jolly Beggars*—a narrative in verse, within set lyrics—his ruffianly cast of drabs and drunkards, of tinkers, fiddlers, and tattered old soldiers, deny the validity of law, the virtue of decorum; they mock the conventions and sanctions and tedious observances of organised society; and brazenly assert, not the rights, but the sheer delights of the ragamuffins' world in which they choose to live. It is a poem of glowing and exuberant power that goes rollicking to its anarchic conclusion:

> *A fig for those by law protected!*
> *Liberty's a glorious feast!*
> *Courts for cowards were erected,*
> *Churches built to please the priest.*

In his *Epistle to Dr Blacklock*, however, he declares:

> *To make a happy fireside clime*
> *To weans and wife,*
> *That's the true pathos and sublime*
> *Of human life.*

And his long poem called *The Cotter's Saturday Night*—a mawkish, sanctimonious piece—was evidently written out of a sincere, though passing, belief that domestic virtue, preferably in humble surroundings, was the summit of human achievement.

There are two sides to a penny, and like a penny Robert Burns can show opposite faces. He wanted to be a rake and a libertine, he wanted also to be a good husband and a kind father. He was for king and country, and for revolution too. He was a poet of indisputable genius, but openly enjoyed the most general pleasures. He could write, with manifest sincerity, 'What signifies the life o' man, An' 'twere na for the lassies, O!' And then, as readily and whole-heartedly, he would gratefully recognise the significance of Scotch drink:

> *Fortune! if thou'll but gie me still*
> *Hale breeks, a scone, an' whisky gill,*
> *An' rowth o' rhyme to rave at will,*
> *Tak a' the rest!*

But Fortune was kinder than that. In Robert Burns Fortune found, and gave to Scotland, the ideal folk-hero.

Off the Atlantic coast of Scotland there rise from the ocean innumerable islands, large and small, that look like crumbs from a geological cake which, in the slowness of geological time, has been drifting eastwards. Beyond its northern coast the archi-pelagos of Orkney and Shetland resemble erratic stepping-stones towards the gale-swept Faeroes and the snow-on-lava grimness of Iceland. All these islands are important. On some of them can be traced the passage of the megalithic builders who came out of the Mediterranean, who left their memorials in Ireland and the long island of Lewis, and raised in Orkney their master-work, Maeshowe. The islands have their own beauties, their own histories. Shetland and Orkney were essential stages for the Viking invasions of Scotland, Ireland, and England which, after two hundred years of sporadic warfare led to, and made possible, the Norman conquest of England. That holy scrap of an island, Iona beyond the Ross of Mull, was Columba's landfall, and from Iona the Christian message—of hope in the darkness of heathendom, of learning in the deserts of ignorance—was carried to Northumbria when Northumbria was the heart and brain of England, and thence to the pagan south of England and a pagan continent. Fisherman and ornithologist, geologist, archaeologist, and botanist can all find material for their books in the islands of the west and north; but their stories are too various to be neatly attached to a perspective view of the mainland.

Even in that restricted view there are faults—in the geological sense—and failure to see all that should be seen. . . .

Many years ago I walked to the western end of Loch Rannoch, which points with a sort of terrible finality to the illimitable peat-hags, rock, and water of that wilder-ness, the Moor of Rannoch; and being young, foolish, and full of energy I turned north, to walk farther, under Ben Alder, up the west side of Loch Ericht to Dal-whinnie on the main road from Perth to Inverness. It rained all that day, with a windless, solid descent, and I remember the long march for two reasons. The more emotional is that never, even in a bath, have I *felt* so wet; the other, which is more interesting, is that on the drenched and plodding shore of Loch Ericht I made a plan, or told myself, that in the near future I would walk by every major loch in Scotland, and chronicle minutely all I saw and did: what birds I noticed, what fish I caught, what shepherds, gamekeepers, solemn anglers or casual visitors I met, and what they told me. And did I do anything of the sort? Nothing! Nothing at all.

Just as there are gaps in this narrative which may well earn me individual readers' rebukes, so there are great lochs in Scotland that rebuke me for unforgivable neglect: Loch Lomond, the greatest of all, splendid under its hill, and many-islanded; Loch Awe, under Ben Cruachan, with sombrely romantic, ruined castles on its little islands; Loch Katrine, idyllic and utilitarian too: it supplies the thirsty city of Glasgow with water, and it gave Walter Scott a *mise-en-scène* for his long poem, *The Lady of the Lake*. There is Loch Leven, the sad periphery of Queen Mary's imprisonment, but much esteemed by fishermen; there are Loch Maree, under the cliffs of Slioch, and Arkaig by the hills where the Young Pretender walked in desperation. There is dark Loch Hourn, there are all the sea-lochs of the west, and in the Ettrick Forest St Mary's Loch, which William Wordsworth, in one of his old-sheep-like moods, declared to be 'visibly delighted' by its surrounding scenery. A very good commentary on Scotland, its past and present, could be written in a series of circumnavigations about its lochs.

The only *lake* in Scotland is the Lake of Menteith in Perthshire; which is a county of many distinctions. Of its hill-lands there are at least fifty peaks that reach a height of more than 3,000 feet, and its great river, the Tay, is fed by such noble streams as the Lyon and the Tummel, Bran, Isla, Almond, and Earn. Its glens are handsome, its lowlands rich, and the passes of Birnam, Killiecrankie, and the Trossachs are famous—almost, indeed, notorious—for their beauty.

Perth, the county town, lies by the river Tay and is uncommonly well endowed with open spaces. The broad meadows of the North Inch and the South Inch used to be islands, when the river, presumably, ran in several channels through undrained marshes, and Perth was a sea-port. In 1313, when Robert the Bruce was steadily winning his war of independence, Perth was still held for the English. Except on its river side, it was defended by a stone wall and a moat; and on a black night in January the king led his army to the attack. Wading through water that reached his chest, he carried a light scaling-ladder, and was the second man over the wall. The garrison surrendered, and the wall was demolished.

Before the end of the century the North Inch was the scene of a remarkable trial by ordeal. The Highland clans had profound objections to a dominating central authority, and from time to time resented their neighbours' activities. They were no more quarrelsome than the great Lowland families—probably less so—but some of their feuds and small campaigns were decorated with spectacular detail or occurred in romantic surroundings, and it became conventional to suppose that Highlanders were always fighting. In the 1390's there was very bitter feeling between two confederacies known as Clan Chattan and Clan Kay, and after much dissension it was decided to settle the dispute by formal combat: thirty chosen men of Clan Chattan would meet, and fight *à outrance,* thirty men of Clan Kay.

The king and his government, to whom all Highlanders appeared as trouble-makers, welcomed the prospect. With any luck, they thought, the population of the Highlands would be reduced by the death of nearly sixty formidable warriors; so preparations were made for the battle to be fought on the North Inch in presence of the king, the elderly and incompetent Robert III, and many of his nobles. Armed with sword and shield, or axe and dagger, the chosen clansmen faced each other, and the battle was about to begin when the chief of Clan Chattan saw that he was a man short. Someone had been assailed by prudence. The chief called for a volunteer, and promised to reward him; whereupon a well-known citizen of Perth, a bow-legged smith called Hal of the Wynd, offered his sword and service for 'half a French crown'; or so says Walter Scott.

The royal trumpets sounded, and the slaughter began. The story is told by Scott in *The Fair Maid of Perth*, and his description of the battle as 'tumultuous chaos, over which the huge swords rose and sank, some still glittering, others streaming with blood', approaches reality, perhaps, as nearly as a modern imagination can go. It is very difficult to visualise the effects of massed sword-play, and quite impossible to assess the capacity of primitive Highlanders to accept wounds and mutilation; though one knows that primitive people have an astonishing tolerance of injury, and even gross injury may not be disabling. According to Scott, ten of Clan Chattan survived the fighting, as well as Hal of the Wynd, but all Clan Kay were killed except one, who escaped by swimming the river. In another account it is said that seven of one side survived, two of the other. There has been much argument and little agreement about the identity of Clan Chattan and Clan Kay, and Hal of the Wynd may have been no citizen, but another Highlander. There is, however, no doubt that the battle was fought. The earliest account of it is by Wyntoun, prior of Loch Leven, who wrote between 1420 and 1424: within, at longest, twenty-eight years of the affray. The records of Perth, moreover, show that 'the erection of the lists' cost £14. 2s. 11d.

In 1437 violence returned, and James I was murdered in the monastery of the Black Friars. By some he had been denounced as a tyrant, but the truth seems to be that he tried to establish the crown's authority and enforce law and order. For some time, moreover, taxation had been in abeyance, but James re-introduced it; and in the circumstances of the time perhaps invited death.

Then, in 1559, John Knox provoked a riot by a sermon he preached in the church of St John. He was 'vehement against idolatry', and in the excitement he aroused the Charterhouse and the houses of the Black Friars and the Grey Friars were all sacked. The County Buildings now occupy the site of Gowrie House, where an Earl of Gowrie tried to kidnap or murder James VI: so said James himself, but as the only consequence of the plot was the convenient death of Gowrie and his brother, the king's word has sometimes been doubted. That was in 1600, and since then Perth has been a more peaceful place.

A dozen miles north and west of it is the charming village—or, if one prefers to call it so, the cathedral city—of Dunkeld. The cathedral, a ruin partially restored, was founded in the 12th century, and the Tay runs close beside it. In Cathedral Street are the little houses of Dunkeld which, to the admiration of all who see them, have been restored by the National Trust. Above the valley of the Tay the country rises fairly steeply, and a few months ago, on a bare hillside not far from Dunkeld, I watched with total fascination what may be called a native ballet. I had risen long before daylight, and my host had driven me, in a Landrover, up a road both rough and steep. We concealed the Landrover, and in the darkness, which very gradually grew paler, we waited for the dancers. When first they came we could hardly see them. They were visible only because their wings and tails seemed to wear a white lining.

They were blackcock: male birds of the sort that old Osgood Mackenzie of Inverewe had killed without thought for the future. They had come to display themselves on what is called a 'lek'—a stage for their ballet—and as the sky lightened their running and leaping became a vivid demonstration of arrogance, agility, and formal aggression. They are big birds, half as large again as a red grouse, and their glossy black coat wears at one end a red-wattled eye, at the other a forked or lyre-shaped tail. They would meet each other on the lek as if in a charge, and just before the impact leap vertically, and hang fluttering in the still air. Then, low to the ground, their necks thrust stiffly out, looking like small animals rather than birds, they would run with surprising speed. There were about a score of them, and the ballet was continuous. Twice a grey hen— the female of the species—flew in, and begged for attention. But the cocks ignored her. Later in the year they would display before their hens, and coupling would follow. But in the early spring the dance is for cocks only. It is ostentation for the sake of ostentation, and a marvellous performance in the high thin air and the loneliness of the hills.

No more than seven or eight miles from where I watched the blackcocks' ballet I saw, a few weeks later, a performance of that fearful play, *The Duchess of Malfi*, by John Webster. That was in Pitlochry, a popular holiday resort distinguished not only by its scenery, but also by possession of a singularly adventurous repertory theatre. It began life in a tent. It acquired some small promise of prosperity, and built with more solidity. Its management has been clever, its choice of plays eclectic and often unexpected: in its current repertoire *The Duchess* stood at one end, at the other was the impudent structure of *The Little Hut*.

With the friend who had taken me to see the blackcocks on their lek, I watched a drama of reckless vengeance. I heard the implacable Cardinal lament his sister's death: 'Cover her face, mine eyes dazzle. She died young.' And suddenly it occurred to me that nowhere else in Britain could I have seen, within seven or eight miles of one another, those large black grouse displaying, and repertory actors portraying a drama from Jacobean England.

Let Perthshire be granted that distinction as well as its fifty peaks, all over 3,000 feet in height, its rushing rivers, Killiecrankie and the Trossachs, and the battle on the North Inch.

If one were asked to advise a sensitive and intelligent visitor to Scotland on how, most profitably and pleasantly, to spend his time, one would, without even momentary hesitation, tell him to make in the first place for Edinburgh; and after a little thought one might well propose Perthshire for rural delectation. Edinburgh, of course, has no rival. A native Scot will, almost certainly, criticise with acrimony much that has been done to soil and blemish the classical, clear serenities of the New Town; but then, even to himself, admit the pride he feels, and the pleasure that his grateful eyes bestow, when from the Castle he walks a Gothic mile to Holyroodhouse, and a little while later perambulates Charlotte Square, crosses the Dean Bridge, and in Ann Street recalls the robust genius of Raeburn. The sensitive and intelligent visitor, turning his back on the north side of Princes Street, will without reservation admit the gratification of a romantic view, and presently walk eastwards down the elegant simplicity of George Street to look again at Arthur's Seat, that municipal mountain, and the dark rampart of the Salisbury Crags. Edinburgh is splendid and *sui generis*; but, as the Duke of Wellington was too much exposed to portrait painters, so has Edinburgh been too often subject to authors, journalists, and writers of architectural, topographical, and historical gossip.

As a county—as the chosen area for rural visiting—Perthshire would not suffer from over-exposure to public esteem, but could not escape the fiercely competitive claims of a dozen other counties. There are those who would say that he who drives towards the Atlantic, through Wester Ross, and from the height of the road beyond Achnasheen sees under the cliffs of Slioch the long blue trench of Loch Maree, has there, before him, the finest view in Scotland. There are others, treading the plateau of the Cairngorms—granite glinting in the sun and ptarmigan exploding from the thin heather—who will declare that nowhere else does the sky enclose so noble and vast a scene of sculptured emptiness and little, rewarding glimpses, far below, of life still humbly persistent. The gaunt and menacing magnificence of Ben Nevis has its devotees, the glens of Angus can name their *aficionados*. I have heard Loch Eriboll in Sutherland spoken of with rapture, and all the mountainous, sea-split lands of Kintail with ecstasy. Two or three hundred years ago the northern parts of Scotland were still dangerously divided among musically minded but warlike clans, and visitors to-day— if they are sensitive and intelligent—are still likely to elect, for their own preference and pleasure, some particular parcel of the Highland landscape, and defend what they declare to be its manifest superiority with as much heat and devotion as if they were MacLeans or MacLeods, Mackenzies, Munros, or Mackays who, in the old sword-bearing days, were defending its frontiers against traditional enemies. It is, then, with a quite false assumption of courage that I choose Perthshire as the county to be favoured by a visitor whose passport unfairly restricts his travel.

To defend my choice I must declare my interest; and that, very briefly, is that through a peasant's eye I prefer a rustic scene to any urban environment that has less than Edinburgh's sublime combination of the Gothic and the Classical. I dote on mountains, white-hooded lochs in a gale of wind, and brawling, honey-hued Highland streams. The green of young larches, the green of shallow seas on a bottom of white sand, and the old green, as of faded kilts, of a Border hill in late October are to me pleasures whose impact never diminishes. There may be significance in the fact that in some of the wildest, farthest, and most arrogantly isolated parts of Scotland its best whiskies are made: Highland Park in Orkney, Lagavulin in Islay, Talisker in Skye, the superlative Glenlivets in that noble intermediacy between hills and the sea that separates the upland parts of Aberdeenshire and Banffshire from the dancing waters of the Moray Firth. In spite of Edinburgh, whose urbanisation grows regrettably, and other towns and expanding cities in the middle of Scotland, I see the knuckle end of Britain as its last part to defy industrialism, suburbanism, over-crowding, and the slow poisons of commercial traffic.

Now the main road through Perthshire, which is the highway to the north, can be uncomfortably congested in the summer months when tourist traffic meanders slowly along a cattle-drovers' route that was never designed for speed. But on the minor roads there is constant pleasure and delight as the view changes from stark hillside to glittering passages of the Tay, the Tummel, the Garry or the Tilt; and the ear responds, as quickly as the eye, to the great resounding names of Balquhidder and Breadalbane, and the winding glens of Errochty and Lyon. In parts of Perthshire there is comfort sufficient for anyone; in others, no more than a few miles from comfort, a grandiose desolation. Scotland is rarely dull, and Perthshire never dull. If one can imagine a traveller—sensitive and intelligent—whose visit to Scotland is irrationally restricted to one half-hour in a city, and one half-hour in a country district, I would, after painful and exhaustive thought, recommend Charlotte Square in Edinburgh, and the Pass of Killiecrankie in Perthshire.

ERIC LINKLATER

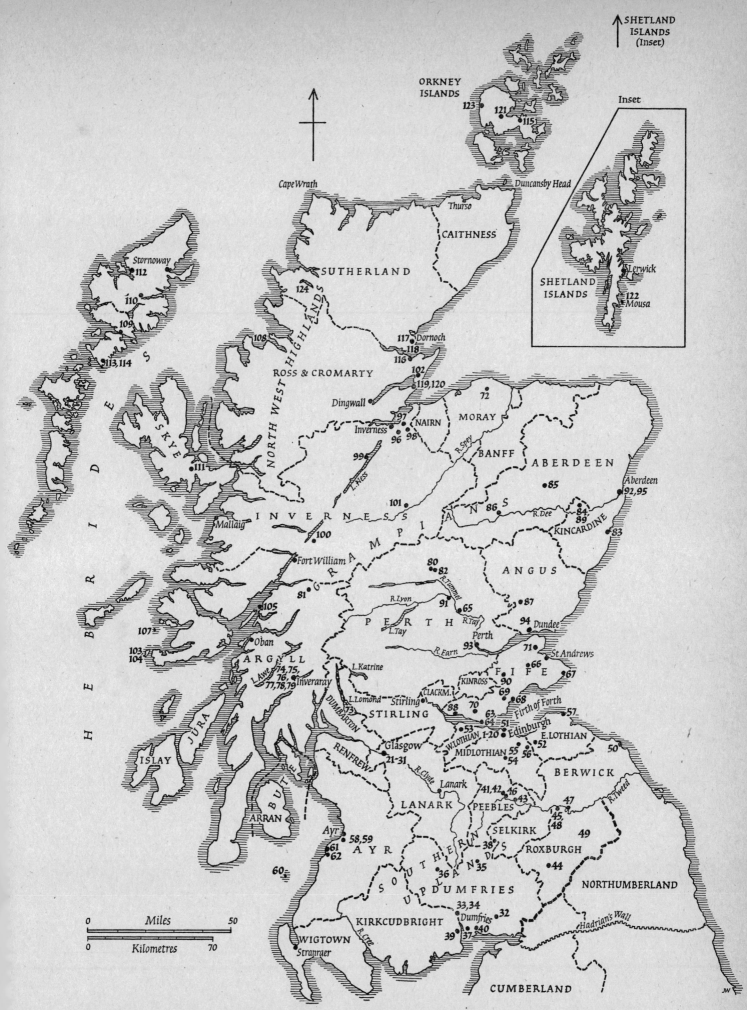

SHETLAND
ISLANDS
(Inset)

ORKNEY
ISLANDS
123 121
115

Inset

SHETLAND
ISLANDS

Lerwick

122
Mousa

Cape Wrath   Duncansby Head

Thurso

CAITHNESS

Stornoway
112   SUTHERLAND

124

110

109   117 Dornoch
108   118
                                       116
                                       102
213, 114   ROSS & CROMARTY   119, 120

                      Dingwall   72

                         97
SKYE   Inverness NAIRN   MORAY

                      96 98
                   99   BANFF   ABERDEEN

111   Aberdeen
                                                              92, 95
                      101   M P I A N   85
                                                          86   S   R. Dee   84
                   Mallaig   89
INVERNESS   KINCARDINE   83
                   100
                                                      80   ANGUS
           81   G R A M   Fort William   82
105   R. Lyon   R. Tummel
                                         91   65   87
107   P E R T H   R. Tay   94 Dundee
103   L. Tay   Perth
104   Oban   R. Earn   93   71
                                                     66   St Andrews
           ARGYLL   L. Katrine   F I F E   67
     L. Awe 74, 75,   KINROSS 90
        76,   69
Inveraray 77, 78, 79   CLACKM. 68
                   L. Lomond Stirling   70   Firth of Forth
                   73   88   63   57
              STIRLING   53 64 51 Edinburgh
ISLAY JURA   Glasgow   W. LOTHIAN 1-20   E. LOTHIAN
                   RENFREW 21-31   MIDLOTHIAN 55 52
                          R. Clyde   54   56   50
ARRAN   Lanark   BERWICK
                              41, 42 16
                                   43   47   R. Tweed
                         LANARK PEEBLES 45
                              38 S   SELKIRK 48 49
       Ayr 58, 59
         61   36   N   35   ROXBURGH
         62   S O U T H E R N D   44
     60   NORTHUMBERLAND
                      U P D U M F R I E S
                              33, 34
         Miles   Dumfries 32
0   50   KIRKCUDBRIGHT   40
                                   39 37
         Kilometres   R. Gree   Hadrian's Wall
0   70   WIGTOWN
         Stranraer

                              CUMBERLAND   JW

The numbers on the map refer to the Plates and corresponding Notes

Part One EDINBURGH AND GLASGOW

Part One EDINBURGH AND GLASGOW

1

2

3

4

7

8

9

10

12

13

14

15

16

17

19

18

20

LONDON — GLASGOW

21

22

25

26

1 THE SCOTT MONUMENT, PRINCES STREET GARDENS, EDINBURGH

Sir Walter Scott died in 1832 and the foundation stone of his extravagant monument was laid eight years later. It was designed by George Meikle Kemp who was described in the *Edinburgh Evening Courant* of 10th October, 1825 as 'an humble artist, not far removed from the position of an ordinary workman, residing in Canning Place, a somewhat obscure street in the southern suburbs of the city'. With its profusion of arches, niches, clustered shafts and soaring pinnacles darkly surrounding his white, robed and seated figure, this Gothic structure exactly suits the author of the Waverley Novels. The figures in the niches represent characters in the novels, while the decorative details of the structure are based on those of a building Scott passionately admired and which inspired some of the most atmospheric passages in his prose and poetry, Melrose Abbey. The marble statue of the writer and his dog Maida was the work of Steell. The monument rises to a height of one hundred and eighty feet and dominates the centre of Edinburgh, marking the division between the Old Town and the New, a fantastic contrast to both the essentially 17th-century character of the former and the classical serenity of the latter, and yet profoundly harmonising with the romantic spirit and spectacular setting of this northern capital.

2 ADVOCATE'S CLOSE, OLD TOWN, EDINBURGH

Blocks of flats or tenements such as these are typical of the Old Town of Edinburgh; they are an ancient institution, originally known as 'lands', perhaps because they were a substitute for land outside the city's bounds—defined by a wall erected after the death of James IV at Flodden—on which the people occupying the area immediately below the castle felt it unsafe to build. As the population increased storey was piled upon storey to a height that made Edinburgh unique among the cities of Europe. The round staircase turrets of these early tenements, well illustrated here, are a vernacular feature derived from tower-house design.

An interesting aspect of the lands was that they housed the nobility and the artisan under the same roof and encouraged a spirit of comradeship and conviviality among the tenants; parties were commonly given to those who shared the same stair. David Hume lived successively in two such tenements, first in Riddle Court and later in the western block of James's Court (subsequently destroyed by fire) in the flat where Boswell entertained Dr Johnson. It is in the closes and courts off the Lawnmarket (the place where the 'landward' or country people had their stalls on market days), especially in those which have not been restored, that the harsh, forbidding and yet romantic atmosphere of the Old Town is most potent. The ghost of John Knox haunts the area; it is the visual expression of the spirit which produced that memorable and horrifying study of fanaticism *The Confessions of a Justified Sinner*. That spirit still lingers in battered corners of the Old Town such as Advocate's Close, for wandering there one dark, misty autumn day the present writer came upon these remarkable lines scribbled in chalk on a peeling door:

Thier arms
are knives thier
Fingers all Nails
When they try to make
love to each other
they drag themselfs
Over miles of broken
glass and stone themselfs
with false confessions.

3 Looking up the Vennel from the Grassmarket

An extension of the city wall (*see* previous note) ran up the Vennel and a portion of this extension still exists alongside Heriot's Hospital, which fronts onto the Grass-market, at the bottom of the steps. The Grassmarket, an oblong open space lying in a hollow below the Castle, was the largest open space in medieval Edinburgh and remained the agricultural market until comparatively recent times. It was the city's place of execution until almost the end of the 18th century.

4 Edinburgh from Salisbury Crags

We are looking across the smoke-veiled, silhouetted roofs of central Edinburgh to-wards the picturesque outline of part of the Royal Mile, the ridge along which ran the high, exposed street which was the nucleus of Edinburgh and which marked the once royal progress from the Castle to Holyrood. It begins with the Castle on its high rock; its second component, the Lawnmarket with its wynds (open alleys) and closes (blind alleys) is roughly contained between the tall Gothic Revival spire of Tolbooth St John's and the exotic crown-shaped steeple of St Giles's Church; the continuation of the Royal Mile, through High Street, can be identified here by the classical steeple of Tron Kirk, named after the Tron, the public weighhouse, which once stood near by. The dome in the middle distance, to the left of the Castle, belongs to the old Quad of the University or King James's College, as it was called. The design, originally by Robert Adam, was altered by William Playfair, commissioned to complete the building after 1815.

5 THE VENNEL, LOOKING ACROSS THE GRASSMARKET TO THE CASTLE
Most cities possess one particular building which stands out as the embodiment of their character and history, but it would be difficult to name a monument which symbolises a city as strikingly as the Castle epitomises Edinburgh. Its image on its high crag hovers over both the Old Town and the New, now poised above roof tops, now, with equally dramatic effect, closing a street vista of medieval irregularity or classical breadth; it, in turn, commands a bird's-eye view of all Edinburgh, the wide, gleaming inlet of the Firth of Forth and the green coast of Fife.

Architecturally the Castle is a collection of buildings of various periods, none of them outstanding, but all contributing to a splendidly evocative whole. The oldest is St Margaret's Chapel, dating from *c.* 1090. It is not visible in this photograph, which shows the Great Hall built by James IV at the beginning of the 16th century, with beneath it the so-called Casemates, huge vaulted chambers used as prisons until the time of the Napoleonic wars. The turretted, battlemented building is the old Palace in which James VI (James I of England), son of Mary, Queen of Scots, was born. It was altered and heightened when the king paid a visit to his native land in 1617.

6 GREYFRIARS CHURCHYARD WITH THE CHURCH OF TOLBOOTH ST JOHN'S
A Franciscan monastery stood here until it was savaged by Argyll and his Reformers in 1559. It was subsequently replaced by the late 16th-century Greyfriars Kirk which is famous for the signing there of the National League and Covenant in 1638, to uphold the Presbyterian form of worship, some of the names being written in blood. The graveyard is one of the most secluded and poetic places in Edinburgh, rich in tombs of the past three hundred years and deep in the clutch of luxuriant ivy. Among the tombs is that of the painter Allan Ramsay (1686-1758). The celebrated Edinburgh photographer David Octavius Hill was strongly attracted by the atmosphere of Grey-friars Churchyard and made its monuments familiar by using them as backgrounds to

75

many of his best-known figure compositions and portraits. (In his day photographers had not begun to use artificial light and it was not possible to make long exposures indoors.)

7 THE SITE OF THE OLD NORTH LOCH BELOW THE CASTLE AND BETWEEN THE OLD TOWN AND THE NEW, SEEN FROM THE ROOF OF JENNER'S STORE

The Old Town of Edinburgh was formerly protected on the north side, below the Castle, by a valley and a loch which effectively prevented the expansion of the city in that direction. The draining of the Loch, begun in 1759, was the first step in the realisation of the daring, imaginative plan for a New Town which had been put forward in 1752 in the *Proposals for carrying out certain Public Works in the City of Edinburgh*: 'to enlarge and beautify the town, by opening new streets to the north and south, removing the markets and shambles and turning the North Loch into a canal with walks and terraces on each side'.

The expense of these public works was to be defrayed by a national contribution. But the extraordinary and fascinating thing about these proposals is not only that the scheme they outlined was actually carried out, but, still more remarkable, that, although it was largely implemented in the first place through the determination of the influential George Drummond, Lord Provost of Edinburgh for most of the 'fifties and part of the 'sixties, the brilliant success of the plan was due to the single-mindedness with which successive Town Councils kept the objectives of the *Proposals* before them for close on a hundred years. It is to them that we owe one of the most magnificent urban developments of the Georgian period and one of the most exciting architectural contrasts in Europe—the confrontation of the Old Town by the New across the dramatic, dividing gulf of the drained Loch. In 1766 the Council advertised for the submission of plans for the New Town, offering as a reward 'a gold medal, with an impression of the arms of the city of Edinburgh, and the freedom of the city in a silver box'. Six plans were received and the scheme suggested by James Craig, an architect about whom little is known, was adjudged best by the Lord Provost and John Adam, elder brother of Robert and son of William Adam, one of the leading Scots architects of the day.

The Mound, on which the buildings in the foreground stand, is situated between Princes Street, built to provide its houses with a prospect (the Gardens and the abrupt cliff of the Old Town), and the neighbourhood of the Castle. The origin of the Mound was an advertisement of 1782 which informed builders at work on the foundations of the New Town that they might dump earth and rubbish at this point in the deep cleft resulting from the drained Loch. The cost of the carting was partly defrayed by the townspeople. The Mound grew at the rate of many cartloads of earth, rubble, and rubbish a year. The neo-classical buildings which now adorn it make an arresting foil to the lofty Castle behind them. The Royal Scottish Academy on the right, in the Greek Doric style, was designed by William Playfair and completed in 1835. The Scottish National Gallery by the same architect, begun in 1850 and finished only in the year of Playfair's death, 1857, is a more austere and a more nobly proportioned structure with Ionic porticos and pilasters. William Playfair, who played a prominent part in the building of the New Town, was born in London in 1789, the son of a Scots architect.

8 CALTON HILL, EDINBURGH

Like the Castle rock, Calton Hill is visible over most of Edinburgh. From afar it makes a smaller impact, for none of its buildings and fragments of buildings is sufficiently prominent to command so vast a panorama. These scattered buildings echo the insistent Edinburgh theme of contrast, for classical monuments confront the battlemented column of the memorial to Nelson, and the Old Observatory by James Craig, designed like a toy fort with crenellations and a stepped gable, is offset by the domed and pillared Roman Doric New Observatory by Playfair. Playfair was also responsible for the circular monument in the foreground of the photograph, a reproduction of the Lysicrates monument in Athens, which commemorates the scholar Dugald Stewart (1753-1828). In the distance again, the Scott monument opposes its Gothic silhouette to the classical outline of this miniature temple.

9 NORTH BRIDGE, EDINBURGH

In July 1763 the Magistrates and Council of the City of Edinburgh invited tenders for a bridge to be built across the North Loch, the drainage of which at that time was nearing completion. Eighteen months later, 'all Architects and others' were asked to submit plans for the bridge, the successful designer to be rewarded with 'thirty guineas, or a gold medal to that value'. The judges, assisted by 'several other Noblemen and Gentlemen of knowledge and taste in architecture', were presented with seven plans and chose those of David Henderson. But Henderson 'failed in finding Security to execute the Bridge agreeable to his estimates' and in July 1765 a design by William Mylne, with alterations by John Adam, was accepted.

The size of the bridge gives some idea of the engineering problem facing the architect. It was to be 1,134 feet long, almost 70 feet high and 40 feet between the parapets over the three arches. The contract price was £10,140 and it was hoped that at least a quarter of this amount could be raised by public subscription. By the beginning of 1769 the bridge was open to pedestrians, but in August of the same year, it partly collapsed, killing five people. It was finally completed in 1772.

The area once occupied by the North Loch was, until the third decade of the 19th century, laid out in walks and gardens tended by those who owned the houses in Princes Street. Access to the gardens was permitted to 'suitable individuals' on payment of three guineas per annum for a key. The construction of the railway through the gardens of what was formerly 'the handsomest street in Scotland' is an early and glaring instance of what was then and still is called 'progress'. After strong but in the end unavailing protest both from the Town Council and a body called the Princes Street Proprietors, trains began to run from Haymarket to Waverley on 1st August, 1846, Playfair having been commissioned to conceal the railway from the Princes Street drawing rooms by a high stone wall and embankment.

Above the busy scene of bridge, railway, and massed buildings rise the stern crags of Arthur's Seat. The proximity of the city to these savage heights is one of the chief visual pleasures of Edinburgh.

10 THE PALACE AND RUINED ABBEY OF HOLYROOD, EDINBURGH

The story of the foundation of the Abbey is bound up with legend. In 1128 St Margaret's son, David I, built the Abbey for Augustinian Canons on the spot where he had miraculously escaped death on the antlers of a stag when sinfully hunting on a holy day. The name Holyrood was derived from Queen Margaret's cross of ebony, ivory, and silver. The traceried east window which figures prominently in the photograph is not medieval, but was added in the reign of Charles I to the nave; this had been truncated soon after the fanatical Earl of Glencairn had smashed the only altars and statues to survive the depredations of the Duke of Somerset in 1546. The window is therefore an example of Gothic survival. It figured prominently in one of Daguerre's most popular dioramas, shown in London in 1826, and a painstaking, almost photographic oil painting of the chapel done at the same time as the diorama shows the tracery half demolished. Clearly, therefore, it must have been restored since then.

Charles I was crowned in the church and it served the parish of Canongate until James VII converted it into a Chapel Royal in 1688. But almost immediately afterwards news of the arrival of William of Orange in London stirred up an outburst of puritanical frenzy; the church was desecrated by the insensate mob, who even violated the royal vault.

The great window, the roofless nave, its cracked and weatherworn masonry laced by lichen-blotched arcading, and a massive Norman tower are all that remain of the Abbey. Though not particularly impressive as monastic ruins, they enormously enhance the pictorial interest of the scene. The shattered hulk of the church with its high gable, its pinnacles and the irregular outline of its crumbling walls throws into sharp relief the classical symmetry of the Palace façade and at the same time intensifies the mood of desolate grandeur encouraged by the bold, dark shape of Arthur's Seat.

The Palace was twice burned down and the present building was completed by Robert Mylne, master mason to Charles II, to designs by Sir William Bruce. Bruce, who in 1671 was appointed 'the King's Surveyor and Master of the Works' in Scotland, had been an ardent supporter of the royal cause throughout the darkest days. As an architect he was described by Colin Campbell in his *Vitruvius Britannicus* as 'justly esteemed the best architect of his time in Scotland'. At Holyrood he repeated the design of the surviving tower at the opposite end of the main front, thus making a symmetrical composition of it, while skilfully transforming the remains of a dour, gloomy structure into a basically classical mansion.

It was in the oldest surviving part of the Palace, dating from about 1500, that those melodramatic scenes were enacted which have made the name of Holyrood so familiar. Here Mary, Queen of Scots lived and here Rizzio was murdered, a brass plate marking the fatal spot.

11 EDINBURGH FROM THE WEST SLOPE OF CALTON HILL

The camera is facing north over the eastern part of the New Town. In the distance lies the Kingdom of Fife across the Firth of Forth and the Forth Bridge. The prominent and handsome Gothic Revival building, twin-towered at either end, is St Paul's Episcopal Church, York Place, built by Archibald Elliot. To the right rises the enormous Gothic pile of the episcopal cathedral of St Mary, designed by Sir Gilbert Scott and consecrated in 1879. The spire in the middle distance belongs to St Stephen's church completed in 1828 to designs by William Playfair.

The presence of this deserted, uncultivated slope in the midst of a great city is as astonishing and gratifying as the contrasts between the Old and the New Town and between the sophistication of the latter and its wild setting.

12 BELLEVUE CRESCENT, EDINBURGH

Bellevue Crescent belongs to the New Town development which took shape between 1803 and 1823. This was controlled by a street plan produced by William Sibbald 'the Good Towns Superintendent of works' and Robert Reid, the architect, and also by a contract, dated 1806, between the City of Edinburgh, the Governors of George Heriot's Hospital and the owners of the land on which the building was to take place; namely, George Winton, James Nisbet, and Thomas Morison, 'Architects of Edinburgh', and Maxwell Gordon and John Morison, Writers to the Signet. Among the many clauses of this contract the following, reprinted in Professor Youngson's *The Making of Classical Edinburgh* (1966), are of great interest in showing how strictly, even at that late date, domestic architecture in the north was still ordered by the rules of taste and proportion first laid down by the Palladians in the previous century.

The contract stipulated that the height of the roof of every house in the different streets 'shall not exceed one third of its breadth' which meant that no roof was to be high-pitched. Further, 'no storm windows nor any raised Breaks in the roof in imitation of French roofs or otherwise shall be allowed'; and 'the sunk storeys shall be of broached ashlar, or rockwork and all above to be polished, droved or broached ashlar, and shall have blocking courses fifteen inches high, and the slates not to project above 3 inches over the said blocking courses'. It was also prescribed that there should be a sunk area in front of each house with a good iron railing in the correct Georgian style.

By the time Bellevue Crescent was built, the simple, compact plan of the earlier Georgian house had been threatened by the introduction of rudimentary plumbing. And though water closets remained the luxury of the few until well on into the 19th century, the contract provided for them with the stipulation that they 'shall not project farther from the back wall than five feet nor be higher than six feet above the level of the parlour floor', thus preventing too great an interruption of the plain symmetry of the rear elevation.

The classical church of St Mary's in the centre of the Crescent was part of the original plan.

13 YORK PLACE, EDINBURGH

York Place, like Elder Street and Duke Street, was built between 1799 and 1804, largely by two local builders, John Reid and John Young. The style followed was much like that seen in Bellevue Crescent except that the severity of the elevation is relieved by round-headed windows on the ground floor. The attics, not permitted by the terms of the contract, were added later. The handsome Gothic lamp standards of cast iron are Victorian.

14 MORAY PLACE, EDINBURGH

Moray Place was designed in 1823 by Gillespie Graham, an architect of humble origin who was born James Gillespie but who, on marrying an heiress, added her name of Graham to his own. Moray Place is truly a *place*, neither a crescent nor a circus, and perhaps the grandest street composition in Edinburgh. It encloses a circular garden with an exciting angular movement, embodied in bold, half-rusticated façades, interrupted by pediments and massive pillars and enlivened by splendid cast iron railings. The late date of this noble group is betrayed only by the large window panes and lack of glazing bars; otherwise it has greater affinities with early Palladian architecture like that of the Woods in Bath than with the stucco villas in the Greek, Castle, or Gothic style which were going up at that time in the south of Britain. The abundance of local building stone and the distance of Edinburgh from the centres of fashion account to some extent for the persistence in Moray Place, with a difference only in degree of magnificence, of the harmony and proportions of the 18th-century squares and terraces of the New Town. But the conditions laid down by the Earl of Moray for the development of his property also encouraged the preservation of the Palladian rules, as the following extract shows: 'That the feuars on the north side of the property and in the east and south of Moray Place will be taken bound to keep the back elevation of their respective houses of the heights and on a level with the front elevation, and to build them of neat, hammer-dressed stone, laid in regular courses with belts and breakings, and a cornice and block course on the top, as shown by the elevations; that the windows in the back of these houses must be placed in a regular and uniform order, and according to the elevations furnished by the said James Gillespie or other architect to be appointed as aforesaid: and it must be understood that no projections from the back of the houses shall be allowed higher than nine feet from the level of the ground.'

The purchasers were to enclose the areas in front of their houses with iron railings 'in a suitable and handsome manner' and were to take upon themselves the whole burden of maintaining the gardens, the houses, pavement, sewers, parapet walls, and streets connected with the development 'to the satisfaction of the said Earl', who was to be put to no expense. The Earl built a house for himself in Moray Place, No. 28.

15 No. 6 CHARLOTTE SQUARE, EDINBURGH. VESTIBULE CEILING
In the first volume of *The Works in Architecture of Robert and James Adam* published in 1773, the two brothers pride themselves on having 'adopted a beautiful variety of light mouldings, gracefully formed, delicately enriched and arranged with propriety and skill'. This ceiling, so much more diffuse and refined than the heavy, compartmented designs which had preceded it, is typical of the style described by the Adams and associated with their name, and fully justifies their claim. The plasterwork is distinguished by several favourite Adam motifs such as the anthemium, the wheat-ear drop, the guilloche, the patera and the garland.

16 NORTHUMBERLAND STREET, EDINBURGH. DOORWAY
Northumberland Street belongs to the same development as Bellevue Crescent, and though built after Robert Adam's death, shows his influence in every detail. The engaged columns; the treatment of the Greek Ionic capitals, which exactly resemble those on the façade of the Royal Society of Arts building in the Adelphi, London; the omission of the architrave from the entablature, so that the frieze rests directly on the abaci of the columns; and the ornamentation of the frieze with paterae and a classical head in relief—all these are characteristic of the Adam style, even though the fanlight is rather simpler, less graceful and web-like than those designed by the master himself.

17 CHARLOTTE SQUARE, EDINBURGH

When the Edinburgh Town Council invited Robert Adam to design Charlotte Square in 1791, he was approaching the end of his life and was at the height of his powers. Carried out in stone instead of the brick and stucco which characterise Adam's town houses in the south, the composition has a solidity which is not usually associated with its author's name. Yet it is light, elegant and even gay by comparison with many other squares and terraces in the New Town. It is conceived in the Palladian tradition, each side of the Square being treated as a single, unified, pedimented façade, and differs from earlier examples of the Georgian terrace, such as Queen Square, Bath or later instances such as Moray Place, in detail rather than form. Adam's façade is enriched with balustrades, festoons and circular panels; and instead of the solemn square doorheads and pedimented windows of the Bath elevations, he has varied his sequences of plain, square-headed openings with graceful Venetian windows and broad, arched doorways. Only the north side of the Square was finished before Adam's death in 1792. It is the most complete example of his street architecture to survive and is almost unique in retaining its original lamp standards with their glass bowls.

18 HILLSIDE CRESCENT, EDINBURGH

Hillside Crescent was designed by William Playfair in 1821 as part of the later development of the New Town. It belonged to a scheme for a crescent 'of great size' on the slopes of Calton Hill, with streets radiating off it to make an impact rather like that 'long felt and acknowledged particularly in the Piazza del Popolo at Rome'. The architecture is ponderous and over-emphatic beside Adam's lively treatment of Charlotte Square, and monotonous when compared with the massive yet unexpected rhythms of Moray Place. The classical style has here hardened into an austere, heavy version of the Doric Order in which the only refreshing touch of fantasy is provided by the charming Greek-key decoration of the railings.

19 ST JOHN'S CHURCH, EDINBURGH. THE VAULT OF THE NAVE

The church, at the west end of Princes Street, was designed by William Burn and completed in 1818. Burn was the son of the Edinburgh builder who had designed the Nelson monument on Calton Hill, and like Playfair had worked in Wyatt's office in London. The pretty fan vault of St John's is carried out in plaster in the light-hearted spirit which informed the revived Gothic of the Regency period. It may be compared with Francis Johnston's vault in the Chapel Royal, Dublin Castle, where as at St John's the proportions of the church are essentially classical despite the Gothic detail and decoration.

20 UPPER LIBRARY, THE UNIVERSITY, EDINBURGH. INTERIOR

The shell of the University is Adam's design, but the interior is the work of Playfair, completed in 1827. The fine pillared vista, opening from either extremity of the long, galleried, rectangular upper floor, immediately recalls that of another famous library, the one designed by Wren at Trinity College, Cambridge. One marks the beginning of the belated Renaissance of classical architecture in Britain, the other sublimely ushers in its last phase. Originally the upper library was to have been furnished at either end with a circular and an outer room, the circular chambers to form domed galleries. The alteration of the plan to make one huge oblong of the area was suggested by Robert Hamilton, Professor of Public Law, who is therefore partly responsible for the present magnificent composition. Today it is no longer in use as the University Library.

21 CENTRAL STATION, GLASGOW

The iron and glass roofs almost universally adopted for railway termini in the last century derived from green-house construction. The finest and most original of these glass-houses is the Palm House at Kew, by the engineer Richard Turner and the architect Decimus Burton, built 1844–8. This vast crystal hall, striped with the wiriest of white iron bars, takes the memorable shape of an ogee curving right down to a low base. The great Crystal Palace by Paxton which followed was a triumph of engineering, but assumed as far as possible the Gothic style which its author passionately admired. The cathedral-like form of the Crystal Palace and the whole revivalist trend of Victorian architecture powerfully influenced the design of railway stations, so that these functional buildings, making such brilliant use of new materials, are usually aisled beneath roofs which ape the king and queen post and even the hammer-beam construction of the Middle Ages, while the columns are graced with Gothic capitals and the spandrels of the arches are filled with cast iron tracery. Central Station, which dates from the late 'seventies, when the Caledonian Railway was brought into the heart of the city, and which displays massive steel tie beams and prominent queen posts overhead, is remark- able for the plainness of its columns and for its departure from Gothic example in its ingenious use of the fanlight motif in its walls: the giant, semicircular web patterns that fill the wholly iron and glass upper stages of the structure sharply contrast with the domestic scale of the twin round-headed lights of the ground floor openings. The extremes of Victorian achievement are forcefully exemplified by this utilitarian yet adventurous building and its neighbour, the station hotel, erected at the same time in a bastard Netherlandish style.

22 QUEEN STREET STATION, GLASGOW. CAST IRON CAPITAL

While the materials used, steel, cast iron, and glass, are entirely of the industrial age, the design of this capital harks back to earlier architectural traditions. It is none the less an astonishing piece of imagery, for it combines a version of the Roman Corinthian capital with an abacus ornamented with the Norman nail-head motif. The decoration marking the intersection of the steel truss is distinctly Gothic in flavour. The high quality and precision of the cast iron detail remind us that Glasgow is still renowned for its ironwork.

23 QUEEN STREET STATION, GLASGOW

Here the ornate capital of the previous photograph can be seen in its setting of glass and iron. Except for its exotic columns, this station departs more radically from the ecclesiastical tradition than Central Station. The vast span of the central rectangle is supported by a light, simple and absolutely functional steel truss and its breadth is emphasised by the treatment of the glass filling the huge, shallow arch of the inner end as a simple display of thin, repeating panels.

The photograph was taken on a Bank holiday and the family groups on the platform are out for a day's excursion.

24 GLASGOW FROM THE NECROPOLIS

The 19th-century Necropolis on its hill, looking across the smoke-hazed silhouette of the city and the valley of the Clyde to Rutherglen and Lanarkshire, is one of the few places in Glasgow where the vigorous hum of raw, teeming life is hushed. The graveyard lies behind the Cathedral and was the old Fir Park of the bishops. It abounds in curious architectural conceits, among them the Menteith Mausoleum of 1842 by David Cousin, based on the Mausoleum of Galla Placidia in Ravenna; a slender domed and battlemented hexagon in the Moorish style, known as the 'Kiosk', commemorating the traveller William Rae Wilson; and the conspicuous monument to Knox by Thomas Hamilton, dated 1825 and taking the form of a Doric column supporting a statue of the Reformer.

The predominantly neo-Greek character of the Necropolis, interrupted by oddities, is in key with the atmosphere of this whole extraordinary city. Although its history by no means begins with the establishment of ship-building and heavy engineering in the mid 19th century, it is with the development of such industries that the name of Glasgow is specially associated. The civic and domestic building which accompanied this industrial expansion is outstanding because at a time when everywhere else Gothic was the most acceptable style, Glasgow architects such as the famous Alexander Thomson and the less well known but brilliant William Stark, David Hamilton and John Stephen were designing churches and terraces in the neo-Greek manner. These classical

84

works were interspersed with such eccentric structures as Templeton's Carpet Factory of polychrome brick with fish-tail castellations, a warehouse which was a replica of the Bargello in Florence and a church (St Margaret's Tollcross) with an Essex village-style clapboard belfry.

25, 26 LAURIESTON HOUSE, CARLTON PLACE, GLASGOW. INTERIOR

Carlton Place is an impressively simple classical terrace with a central pediment facing the Clyde. It was designed by Peter Nicholson and begun in 1802 as part of a planned but never completed scheme of development promoted by John Laurie. The stair-well of Laurieston House gives some idea of the elaborate interiors that lie behind the plain façades of these houses. The name of the plasterer is not known, though he is said to have been an Italian and his style has close affinities with that of Adam. The frieze of paterae and flutes dividing the two storeys, the roundels containing reliefs of classical figures and trophies of arms, the festoons, arabesques and husk chains are all in the Adam manner. The cast iron balustrade with its anthemion-derived motif is also a simplified version of a type favoured by Adam.

27 GREAT WESTERN TERRACE, GLASGOW

This terrace by Alexander Thomson, begun in 1869, shows the individuality of architecture in Glasgow at a time when almost every new building was influenced by the Gothic Revival style. The composition is extremely simple and yet varies the classical terrace theme in a most original way. A long row of two-storeyed houses is interrupted by massive three-storeyed blocks projecting as far as the coupled Ionic porticos of the two-storeyed units. These porticos, the heavy string course and the wide eaves, quite unlike those of Georgian houses, impart strong, lively chiaroscuro to a design which might otherwise appear coldly drab and severe. A faint hint of the Gothic taste of the day has crept, perhaps unwittingly, into the shape of the arches enclosing the crisp anthemion ornament of the cast iron balustrades.

28 VILLA IN NITHSDALE ROAD, GLASGOW

This single-storeyed villa, also designed by Alexander Thomson, is an even more idiosyncratic example of the talents of this resourceful architect. It is a late (1871), strikingly original and successful expression of the Picturesque cult of exotic styles, taking the form in this northern, industrial city of an Egyptian temple. The long, low massive shape is relieved by chimneys like Egyptian columns with palm leaf capitals and by the gaiety of the cast iron cresting along the eaves.

29 THE SCHOOL OF ART, RENFREW STREET, GLASGOW

This famous building, known all over Europe as a pioneer work of the Modern Movement, was the result of a competition held in 1896. The winning design, chosen from among entries submitted by most of Glasgow's leading architects, was by C. R. Mackintosh. The library block, shown here, was not completed until 1907–9 and by that time Mackintosh had altered his original plans for this wing. The building might well be taken for a product of the most advanced ideas of the 'thirties, but the architect himself sometimes referred to his work as traditional and declared that he drew his inspiration from vernacular architecture. It is indeed just possible to regard the tall narrow windows of the library as elongated oriels, while the bleak expanse of wall to the left, pierced by one tiny window and topped by a steep roof behind a parapet, is certainly reminiscent of Scottish castle architecture. Mackintosh was admired in both Germany and Austria in the first decades of the 20th century and his work influenced the formation on the Continent of a new functional, machine-based aesthetic.

30 THE SCHOOL OF ART, GLASGOW. INTERIOR OF THE LIBRARY

With its plain, insistent vertical posts, rectilinear furniture and complete rejection of the Victorian Gothic style, this unified, uncluttered design anticipates the modern international movement even more conspicuously than the exterior of the building. The only period touch occurs in the spare Art Nouveau decorative detail of the gallery balustrades. The library is particularly important because nearly all Mackintosh's austere, unified interiors have vanished.

31 GLASGOW CATHEDRAL. THE NAVE

The best preserved Gothic building in Scotland stands in its most heavily industrialised city. It is the earliest building of importance in Glasgow and it is a monument to the saint who made Glasgow pre-eminent among the early settlements in the lower Clyde valley despite the more favourable geographical situations of other places. St Mungo lived on the banks of the Molendinar, the stream that flows (though now hidden) through the valley to the east of the church, and the Cathedral grew about his venerated tomb. The first church to be built over the saint's grave was burned in 1192 and the present Cathedral was begun shortly afterwards. The architecture already shows the strong flavour of individuality which distinguishes so many of the later buildings of Glasgow, for although constructed piecemeal at different periods, it is remarkable for the uniformity of its style. Anyone looking at the nave for the first time and knowing nothing of the building history of the Cathedral would take it for an Early English work while commenting on the unconventional design of the plain, deeply cut mouldings of the capitals. But the nave was not completed until 1480, when its style was almost two centuries out of date. It was very unusual for medieval craftsmen to adapt their work to the style of an earlier part of a building, but the Glasgow masons either deliberately built this nave to accord with the beautiful 13th-century chancel, the Early English form of which was already a little behind the times, or they had failed to catch up with the changes which had been going on in the south.

Part Two   THE LOWLANDS

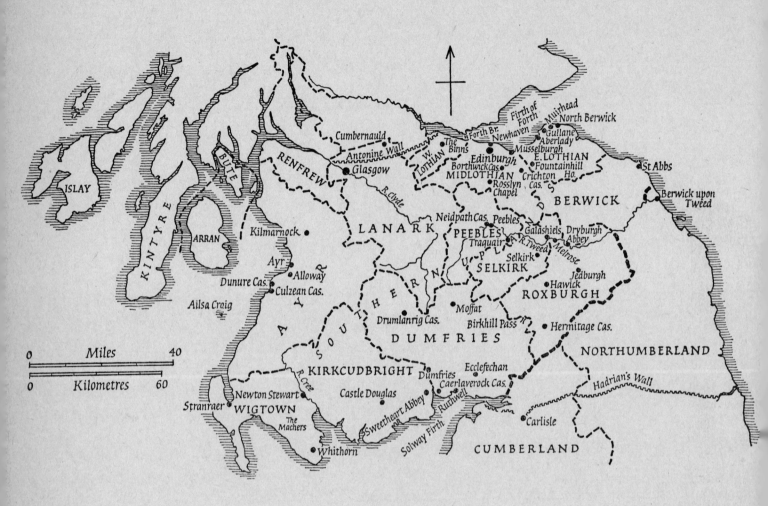

ISLAY

KINTYRE

BUTE

RENFREW

Cumbernauld

Antonine Wall

Glasgow

ARRAN

Kilmarnock

Ayr

Dunure Cas.

Alloway

Culzean Cas.

Ailsa Craig

A Y R

LANARK

R. Clyde

W. LOTHIAN

The Binns

Borthwick Cas.

Edinburgh

MIDLOTHIAN

Rosslyn Chapel

Crichton Cas.

Firth of Forth

Forth Br.

Newhaven

Musselburgh

Aberlady

Gullane

Muirhead

North Berwick

E. LOTHIAN

Fountainhill Ho.

St Abbs

BERWICK

Berwick upon Tweed

Neidpath Cas.

Peebles

PEEBLES

Traquair

Galashiels

Dryburgh Abbey

R. Tweed

Melrose

SELKIRK

Selkirk

Jedburgh

Hawick

ROXBURGH

S O U T H E R N

Moffat

Drumlanrig Cas.

DUMFRIES

Birkhill Pass

U P L A

Hermitage Cas.

NORTHUMBERLAND

KIRKCUDBRIGHT

R. Cree

Dumfries

Ecclefechan

Caerlaverock Cas.

Ruthwell

Hadrian's Wall

Newton Stewart

Castle Douglas

Sweetheart Abbey

Stranraer

WIGTOWN

The Machers

Whithorn

Solway Firth

Carlisle

CUMBERLAND

Miles   0 ——— 40

Kilometres   0 ——— 60

32

33

44

45

47

48

50

54

60

61

63

64

32 THE BIRTHPLACE OF THOMAS CARLYLE, ECCLEFECHAN, DUMFRIESSHIRE
The 'Arched House' was built, probably about 1791, by Carlyle's father and uncle, and the writer was born here in 1795. He is buried in the churchyard of Ecclefechan. The little town is described as Entepfuhl in *Sartor Resartus*.

Although the structure, with its harled or roughcast and whitened walls in the vernacular style, looks almost primitive when compared with Georgian country town houses in the south, it is nevertheless more elaborate and has more pretentions to style than many other small houses built in Scotland at the same time and is a conspicuous object in the single street of Ecclefechan. The strong tradition of single-storey dwellings persisted in country districts throughout the 18th century; it was only the wealthier and gentler classes, merchants, lesser lairds, and the clergy, who enjoyed the luxury of two floors, Georgian symmetry and perhaps some other echo of the Palladian manner. Carlyle's father and uncle were both master masons and this accounts for such details as the crude version of the Venetian window above the arch.

The writer's parents moved to a larger house in the town in 1798, but the Arched House remained in the Carlyle family until 1910 when it was conveyed to the Carlyle's House Memorial Trust.

33 DUMFRIES
The town, an old seaport built largely of the local red stone, is splendidly situated near the mouth of the fast-flowing river Nith. The early history of the town was turbulent, for it was burned and sacked by the English in 1448, 1536, and 1520; before that, in 1306, it was the scene of the murder by Robert Bruce of his rival John Comyn after a quarrel before the altar of a Franciscan church which once stood in Castle Street.

Robert Burns served as excise officer here from 1791 until 1796.

Dumfries is a wool town engaged in the traditional branch of the industry, the weaving of tweeds, the wool for which comes from the Cheviot sheep. Tweeds differ from English worsteds in the way in which the yarn is prepared. With worsted it is combed, the fibres being smoothed and laid parallel to each other, while with tweeds the fibres are deliberately tangled to produce a rougher, livelier texture and a heavier material. Most of the woollen gloves made in Great Britain also come either from Dumfries or Aberdeen.

34 ST MICHAEL'S CHURCH, DUMFRIES

The church, built 1745–54, incorporates classical features in a tower topped by French-derived angle turrets and a broach spire. Burns worshipped here, and a tablet marks the site of his pew. He lies in the churchyard where his somewhat pretentious monument takes the form of a Greek temple with a sculptured group of the Muse Thalia finding Burns at the plough. The churchyard is altogether rich in tombstones and monuments of robust Baroque character, dating mostly from the early 18th century. Three tablets commemorate covenanters who fell victims to 'prelatic rage'.

35 THE FORMER TOWN HOUSE, MOFFAT, DUMFRIESSHIRE

The toy-like character of the neat town of Moffat is well conveyed by this charming little building adorned with Victorian lettering, dating from the time when it was turned into shops, and topped by a square clock tower. The whitewash of the lower stage of this structure gives it an endearingly primitive air. The lettering on the blocked window, which reads, 'Visit the mineral wells and drink the famous water', recalls the days when the present council offices were still *Bath Buildings* and Moffat was still frequented for the celebrated efficacy of its waters in curing 'scrofulous and rheumatic' complaints. A sulphur spring was discovered near the town in 1630, and Moffat reached the height of its prosperity as a mineral spa in the 18th century when Hume, Boswell, and Burns were among those who took the waters.

The town is finely situated at the foot of a wooded, conical hill with mountains on every side but the south.

36 DRUMLANRIG CASTLE, DUMFRIESSHIRE

This exciting building of red sandstone raised up on its high podium is a striking object in the undulating landscape of the Nith valley. It was designed by Sir William Bruce (*see also* pl. 10) in 1675–88 for the first Duke of Queensberry. The name of Bruce is less familiar across the Border than that of his great contemporaries Wren, Hawksmoor, and Sir John Vanbrugh, but he is of their company in the boldness of his imagination. Drumlanrig Castle with its grandly sweeping forecourt, introduced by huge, rusticated ball-topped piers, its crab-pincer perron, fantastic roof line and aspiring, advancing and retreating movement is related in feeling to the great Baroque houses of the Continent such as Pommersfelden and Brühl, and yet Bruce's version of the Baroque has much greater affinities with the Elizabethan synthesis of the vertical and horizontal modes than with either of those German masterpieces. In fact the design of the Scottish mansion, a hollow square with prominent corner towers, at once recalls that of Wollaton Hall, and perhaps Bruce should be regarded as a belated Elizabethan rather than an early Palladian. It is only necessary to glance at the unorthodox width of the entablature above each pedimented window to realise that the architect was not concerned with the letter of the classical rule even though the symmetry and much of the imagery of his composition shows that he grasped the fundamentals of that rule.

Bruce's originality lies in the satisfying way in which he has harmonised classical and traditional motifs in a design as superbly confident as that of the great house with which I have compared it, Wollaton. It is in the roof line that the interest of the composition is concentrated. From the great height of the towers, rendered yet taller by pepper-pot angle turrets, the bays of each façade are graded at different levels, converging in the main front, seen in the photograph, upon a central projecting feature which carries the design upwards again to an open segmental pediment and a cupola on an octagonal drum. The varying roof levels are accentuated by a bold balustrade, the horizontality of which contrasts with the emphatic verticals of turrets and chimneys. And this contrast is set in dramatic motion against the sky by a variety of perspectives, recessions and advances.

Another singular feature of Drumlanrig is the sculptured ornament. Each pediment is crammed with heraldic carving in deep relief, swags of fruit hang about the entrance, and huge trefoils encircle the principal cupola. Pediments often frame sculpture in French buildings, as at Valençay and Serridant on the Loire, but never in such crowded array, and here the ornament is additionally remarkable in having been cut on the spot from the stones of the wall face. Although it does not play the spectacular role which sculpture assumes in the great creations of the Baroque, this carving hints at a fusion with the building itself to foster an impression of vivid contrast and movement.

37 CAERLAVEROCK CASTLE, DUMFRIESSHIRE

In a land of castles the ruins of Caerlaverock, picturesquely situated near the mouths of the Locker and the Nith, are memorable for the impression they leave of a scene of violent destruction rather than gentle decay. And indeed Caerlaverock suffered continually in the Border struggles. Besieged and taken by Edward I, it was later dismantled by Robert Bruce; then, after having fallen again into the hands of the English, it was recaptured and wrecked in the process by Sir Roger Kirkpatrick in 1555. Shortly afterwards it succumbed to the Earl of Sussex and then was recovered by Lord Maxwell, a descendant of its ancient owners. It was he who rebuilt the castle in 1583, adding the domestic structure with its pedimented windows, now rent and roofless, seen to the right of the photograph. The Maxwells inhabited Caerlaverock for a time but in 1640 after a siege of thirteen weeks it was taken by the Covenanters and given up to one Finch who in the receipt for its furniture lists eighty beds, a proof of the former splendour of the castle. But the shattered fortress was no longer tenable and was left to sink into a yet more ruinous state than that already wrought by centuries of fighting.

The tower in the foreground of the photograph with its corbelled parapet and the one glimpsed just behind it were part of the 15th-century gatehouse; it is the contrast in scale and style between these enormous, plain-walled cylinders and the gables, chimneys and richly articulated walls of the house with their sculpture-filled triangular and semi-circular pediments (*see also* pl. 36) which invests these ruins with such a peculiarly intense air of desolation.

38 BIRKHILL PASS, DUMFRIESSHIRE

The pass lies about 20 miles from Moffat on the borders of Selkirkshire near the birth-place of James Hogg. This grandly romantic countryside was the last haunt of the persecuted Covenanters. They had been abjured by Charles II at the Restoration in 1660 and repressive measures grew ever more ruthless in the years that followed. In 1685 adherence to the Covenant was declared treasonable, and during the 'Killing Time' which lasted from 1685 until 1688 the Covenanters were hunted down and slain, often without trial. James Renwick, the last covenanting martyr, executed at Edinburgh on 17th February, 1688, preached for the last time near the burn shown in the photograph. The stream comes from Loch Skeen, a wild, dark lake high in the hills, whence it falls in a single impressive sheet of foam, described by Scott in *Marmion* as 'white as the snowy charger's tail'.

These bleak, furrowed slopes are memorable for their colour and texture: they look as though they were sheathed in a harsh, rusty-green, moth-eaten plush, accentuating rather than softening the stark contours of the heights.

39 SWEETHEART OR DULCE COR ABBEY, KIRKCUDBRIGHTSHIRE

The photograph shows the crossing, the north transept, and part of the choir of the ruined church of the Cistercian abbey founded in 1275 by Devorguilla, wife of John de Balliol. She was buried in front of the High Altar and with her was interred her husband's heart, treasured since his death some years before her own.

The abbey was originally to be a daughter house of Dundrennan. A statute of the Cistercian General Chapter in 1270 commands the abbots of Furness and Rievaulx to inspect the site 'in which the widow of John de Balliol intends to found an abbey of monks'.

The Cistercian Order, which took its name from the abbey of Citeaux in Burgundy, had been founded at the end of the eleventh century as part of a reaction against the decline of the fervour and austerity of early monasticism. The main expansion of the Order in Britain was in the north of England and in the Border country, where there were few monasteries of the older Orders and where vast tracts of wild country accorded with the Cistercian preference for sites remote from towns and with the emphasis this Order placed upon agricultural work. Sweetheart Abbey, like the Yorkshire foundations, belongs to the period when a great increase in the number of recruits to the Order and a corresponding increase in wealth had led to a certain relaxation in the dogmatic severity of early Cistercian architecture. Thus, although St Bernard, Abbot of Clair-vaux, whose zeal and eloquence had done so much to establish the Cistercian Order, had insisted that there was to be no ostentatious tower, the crossing of this church is surmounted by a massive tower some 90 feet high, and chapels open from the eastern sides of the transepts. But though the plan of the church is more elaborate than the simple, aisleless structures of the first Cistercian buildings, the restraining influence of the early compulsory austerity is still felt in the plain mouldings of the piers and capitals, in the reticent tracery of the wheel window and in the impeccable proportions of the elevations which relate this northern foundation to other Cistercian abbeys as distant as Tintern or Abbey Dore, as clearly as do peculiarities of plan such as the character-istic placing of the frater at right angles to the cloister and the insertion of a door in the transept wall (seen in the photograph) leading directly into the cemetery.

The abbey became the property of Sir Robert Spottiswoode in 1924.

40 THE RUTHWELL CROSS, DUMFRIESSHIRE. DETAIL

Fragments of hundreds of carved crosses of the pre-Conquest period are found all over the northern counties of England and the south of Scotland. The Ruthwell Cross is one of the most arresting and celebrated examples of these works. It was flung down and shattered by the Puritans in 1642, reconstructed in 1823, and set up in the manse garden where it remained until 1887 when it was moved into Ruthwell Church. The cross dates from the late 7th or early 8th century, the period when, under the powerful kings of Northumbria, Roman Christianity was displacing the system of St Columba, under which the Picts had originally been converted to the Christian faith. The monu-ment is a monolithic shaft, 18 feet high, with sunk panels on both back and front containing figures in bold relief. The subjects of the panels shown in this detail are

Mary Magdalene wiping the feet of Christ with her hair and, below this, a scene rarely found in the West, of St Paul and St Anthony meeting in the desert. The sides of the shaft are ornamented with vine scrolls and pecking birds. Both this motif and the relief of the two saints recall Syrian and Coptic works of the period and it is not improbable that these carvings, like those on the famous Bewcastle Cross, may have been the work of foreign masons, such as those known to have been employed at Hexham under both Wilfrid and his successor Acca, or of native craftsmen familiar with their style.

While the idea of erecting tall crosses was probably of Celtic origin, for the Columban monks were certainly in the habit of setting up preaching crosses, the Ruthwell Cross could not have been influenced by any of the Irish examples, for these are later in date and the style of the carving is quite different, much less monumental and more descriptive. It seems more likely that the Irish crosses were inspired by the Northumbrian monuments.

The inscriptions round the reliefs on the Ruthwell Cross are in Latin, but the shaft also bears a poem in runic letters, the Dream of the Holy Rood, one of the earliest known specimens of the English language. Here the Cross itself narrates the part it played in the Passion:

> Then the young Hero, Who was mightiest God,
> Strong and with steadfast mind,
> Up to the cross with steps unfaltering trod,
> There to redeem mankind.
> I trembled, but I durst not fail,
> I on my shoulder bare the glorious King.
> They pierce my sides with many a darksome nail
> And on us both their cruel curses fling.

41 NEIDPATH CASTLE, PEEBLESSHIRE

Scotland is probably richer in tower houses than any country in the world and these fortified dwellings form a unique category in the domestic architecture of Britain. Unsettled conditions led to the persistence of towers as an economical type of defended house long after it had become obsolete elsewhere. Tall, small-windowed and parapeted, usually crowned with massive corbelling and often with fantastic turrets and dormers, looming amid trees, or rising from some rocky eminence, the tower house is the most characteristic building of both the Highlands and the Lowlands.

We are here looking up at Neidpath Castle from the River Tweed which at this point runs through a deep, narrow, and well-wooded glen. An impressive silence enhances the effects of desolation and decay. The fortress comprises two tower houses, a tall, narrow structure to which a more imposing and vastly stronger building was added by Sir William Hay in the 15th century. Before that, Neidpath had been the chief residence of the powerful Border family of Fraser, progenitors of the houses of Lovat and Saltoun in the north. The last of the Frasers was the gallant Sir Simon who defeated the English three times in one day at Roslin in 1302. One of his two daughters married a Hay of Yester, the ancestor of the Marquis of Tweeddale, whose family afterwards quartered the arms of the Frasers with their own. The keystone of the arched portal in the courtyard wall shows the strawberry plant or *fraise* of the Norman-French Frasers and the coronet and goat's head of Hay of Yester. The second Earl of Tweeddale was an ardent Royalist, and Neidpath held out longer against Cromwell than any place south of the Forth. It was this Earl who made the central doorway to the castle seen in the lower photograph, cutting through the thickness of eleven feet of wall. He also excavated a noble staircase out of the massive structure, erected stables to the north of the house, and laid out the steep incline above the Tweed with terraced gardens.

In 1686 the Earl of Tweeddale, having become involved in ruinous litigation with the Duke of Lauderdale, sold Neidpath to William Douglas, first Duke of Queens-berry. His son William, first Earl of March, carried out many improvements, planting 'a good store of ornamental trees of all sorts' and creating a grand avenue.

It was the third Earl of March, later Duke of Queensberry, who accomplished the ruin of Neidpath. Instead of residing at the castle or in Peebles as his father and grand-father had always done, Old Q, as he was called, spent his life almost entirely in England, where he was renowned for his folly and extravagance. He took no interest in his estates and perpetrated an act of vandalism at Neidpath from which it never recovered. In 1795 he sold timber from the trees planted by his ancestor, leaving the river banks and the terrain surrounding the castle a barren wilderness. Wordsworth visited the scene of destruction some years later and was moved to write the following well-known sonnet:

> Degenerate Douglas! oh, the unworthy Lord!
> Whom mere despite of heart could so far please,
> And love of havoc (for with such disease
> Fame taxes him), that he could send forth word
> To level with the dust a noble horde,
> A brotherhood of venerable trees;
> Leaving an ancient dome, and towers like these,
> Beggared and outraged! Many hearts deplore
> The fate of these old trees; and oft with pain
> The traveller at this day, will stop and gaze
> On wrongs which Nature scarcely seems to heed:

For sheltered places, bosoms, rocks and bays,
And the pure mountains, and the gentle Tweed,
And the green silent pastures yet remain.

Abandoned by its owner, Neidpath was let to yearly tenants and gradually fell into decay, while the gardens merged with the sheep walks. The bushes and undergrowth which now cover the banks sprang up during the last century.

42 NEIDPATH CASTLE, PEEBLESSHIRE, SEEN FROM THE GATEWAY OF THE RUINED COURTYARD

Owing to the steep drop in the ground on the west side of the building, the entrance leads into the first floor of the house. This was not the original door; that was on the other side of the fortress, in the angle made by the L-shaped design, close to the brink of the cliff. From it a spiral staircase led to the upper floors of the earlier structure. In the 17th century, in the time of the second Earl of Tweeddale, the parapet was roofed in on the north and south sides to form galleries with turrets, apartments rather like the long galleries of Elizabethan houses. On the façade shown here the parapet walk has been left open.

The interior of Neidpath shows the characteristic tower house plan which is like that of a hall house arranged vertically instead of horizontally. The first floor is taken up by the entrance with a room leading off containing a trap opening to a dungeon and a garderobe. The second floor comprises the Great Hall, panelled in the 17th century with a private room adjoining it, while the third floor consists of two bedrooms. These rooms are still habitable, but on the east side the older building shows a series of spectral vaulted floors open to the heavens. Fragments of a fallen wall lie at the foot of the cliff near the river.

43 THE RIVER TWEED BETWEEN PEEBLES AND NEIDPATH CASTLE, PEEBLESSHIRE

The rolling, pastoral landscape is characteristic of the whole of Tweeddale. This beautiful river, clear and full, courses in large curves for most of its length through wooded slopes, sometimes deeply scored by the gashes of tributary streams, sometimes yielding to well-cultivated plains, and surrounded on all sides by the smooth forms of graceful hills, entirely different from the bold, serrated contours of the Highland mountains. In the photograph we are looking towards Wallace's Hill and this country-side, which lay open to the English armies in the past, witnessed some of the more daring exploits of Sir William Wallace, such as are celebrated in the 15th-century verse of Henry the Minstrel. No sheep are to be seen in the photograph, but the ubiquity of sheep in the Tweed valley has given rise to a large-scale woollen cloth industry with centres at Hawick and Galashiels.

44 HERMITAGE CASTLE, ROXBURGHSHIRE

This grim-walled castle, its severity relieved only by a corbelled parapet and tiny, suspicious windows, perfectly harmonises with the bleak, solitary landscape in which it stands, and the character of both is accentuated by the gentle image of the cow and calf. The animals also serve to show the great scale of the building. Hermitage is one of the most formidable of Border castles and was the chief stronghold of the Douglases from 1341 when Sir William Douglas took it from Lord Soulis. A year later Sir Alexander Ramsay, who had been seized by Douglas at Hawick, was starved to death in the castle dungeon. In 1492 the Douglases exchanged Hermitage with the Bothwells for Bothwell Castle above the Clyde. Mary Queen of Scots rode over from Jedburgh to visit Bothwell as he lay ill here in 1566.

The castle dates mostly from the late 14th century. The most unusual features of the rectangular building are the enormous pointed arches between the corner towers on the east and west façades. The south-west tower which juts out so curiously from one corner of the castle, was an extension of the 15th century.

45 MELROSE, ROXBURGHSHIRE

The footbridge, with its delightful play upon the castle drawbridge theme, connects the little town of Melrose, the 'Kennaquhair' of Scott's *Monastery*, with Gattonside on the further bank of the Tweed. A guide-book of 1832 describes the 'wire bridge' as having been recently constructed. In the background rise the Eildon Hills associated with Thomas the Rhymer and not far from Melrose is the Eildon Tree Stone, said to mark the spot where grew the Eildon Tree beneath which Thomas met the Queen of Faery. The poet lived at Ercildoune, now called Earlston, to the north-east of Melrose, and a fragment of his castle, Rhymer's Tower, still stands there. To an English eye the most striking images in this photograph are the dormer windows of the cottage facing the bridge. They take the surprising form, never seen south of the Border, of bays, and represent a development of the one-storey cottage tradition of Scotland, giving the maximum light to an extra floor constructed in the roof.

46 PEEBLES. IRON FOOTBRIDGE

Peebles takes its peculiar name from the *Pebyll* or tents of the Gadeni, the wandering tribe who originally inhabited Tweeddale. Known principally for its tweed mills, it is a grey-brown town set in pastoral, hilly country at the junction of the Tweed and

Eddleston Water. Owing to the nature of its site, Peebles consists of several detached parts connected by bridges. The Tweed is spanned by a picturesque five-arched stone bridge built at the end of the 15th century, while five other bridges cross Eddleston Water. Of these the Victorian cast-iron structure is of minor importance but its pretty criss-cross patterns and the intriguing hint of the Orient about its piers add a welcome note of fantasy to the unremarkable architecture of a town whose ecclesiastical grandeur was laid in ruins at the Reformation and whose domestic buildings include but one outstanding house, the Chambers Institution, dating mostly from the 17th century, formerly the property of the Queensberry family. The footbridge bears the date 1852.

47 DRYBURGH ABBEY, BERWICKSHIRE. THE DOORWAY FROM THE CLOISTER GARTH TO THE NAVE

The ruins are most picturesquely situated on a richly wooded peninsula almost islanded by the Tweed. The abbey was a Premonstratensian foundation of 1150, probably by Hugh de Morville, Constable of Scotland, and received a charter from David I. The canons introduced to it came from Alnwick. The Premonstratensians took their name from Premontré, the monastery of the founder of their Order, St Norbert, who was a friend of St Bernard and shared his austere views. And although they followed the Rule of St Augustine, the Premonstratensians or White Canons organised themselves on the Cistercian model and were influenced by the Cistercians in the design of their churches. The domestic ranges at Dryburgh seem to have been built very largely within fifty or sixty years of the date of the foundation, judging from the style of the remains, while the church was in course of construction during the 13th century. The abbey was twice wrecked by the English, in 1322 and again in 1385; in 1545 it was savagely plundered by the Earl of Hertford, who carried off most of the fittings. The ruined abbey was annexed to the Crown in 1587. Finally it was erected into a temporal barony, with the title of Lord Cardross, in favour of the Earl of Mar, who later sold the property. It passed through several hands and was eventually acquired by the Earl of Buchan in 1786. It was he who assigned to Sir Walter Scott the burial place of his ancestors, the family of Haliburton, one-time owners of Dryburgh. The novelist lies in the east aisle of the north transept.

The doorway leading from the cloister into the nave is an expressive example of the transitional style. The deeply recessed arch is rounded in the Norman fashion and the capitals of the shafts are Norman in shape, but the leaf ornament of these capitals is typically Early English and the prominent dog-tooth moulding of the inner order is one of the commonest motifs of this style. The nave itself presents a scene of dreadful destruction: the piers are all demolished and only traces of the north wall remain: but this does not appear in the photograph, which yields a glimpse through the door of the north transept and choir. Enough survives of this noble structure to show that the simple, elegant design is still controlled by the effects of the earlier insistence of the Order on the dignity of abstract form. Mainly in the Early English style, the rhythm of a very unusual composition is emphasised by the clear lines of perfectly plain mouldings. We are presented with a novel shift of accent in the relation of arcade, triforium, and clerestory; for the triforium, which is generally more prominent than the clerestory, has shrunk to the proportion of a broad band, marked by string courses, between the arcade arches and the arches of the clerestory, which are grouped three to a bay, the central one, opposite to the window, being larger than the side arches. Behind these openings runs a gallery. The triforium arches, on the other hand, assume a form which in a more conventional design would certainly be allotted to the clerestory: they are flat-headed openings filled with huge cusped circles.

48 MELROSE ABBEY, ROXBURGHSHIRE. THE CHOIR

The Cistercian Abbey of Melrose was founded by David I and the church was dedicated on 28th July, 1146. The original monks came from the great Yorkshire abbey of Rievaulx. The 12th-century building no doubt conformed to the austere principles of the Order, but hardly a trace of it remains, for the monastery lay in the direct path of the English invaders and was wrecked many times and with exceptional severity in 1322 under Edward II, and in 1385 under Richard II. Robert Bruce repaired and rebuilt the abbey in 1326 and bequeathed his heart to the church, beneath the high altar of which it is said to have been deposited after an unsuccessful attempt had been made to carry it to the Holy Land. He died at Cardross, near Dumbarton, in 1329, and his body was buried in Dunfermline Abbey.

Little survives at Melrose of Bruce's restoration and the ruins date chiefly from a later rebuilding of the end of the 14th and the early 15th century. The monastery was plundered by the Earl of Hertford in 1545 and was later bombarded by Cromwell from the Gattonside Hills. Before this, in 1608, the abbey had been elevated to a temporal lordship for Viscount Haddington, created Lord Melrose, and from then until 1810 the monks' choir, which included three bays of the nave, was used as a Presbyterian church. In view of its violent history and the fact that the ruins were widely used as a quarry for building-stone, it is astonishing that so much of the structure still stands. Certainly the remains afford sufficient proof of a style which considerably diverges from the simplicity of the Cistercian mode, and which even in decay is remarkable for its elaborate plan and profusion of ornament. The plan is complicated by an extraordinary number of chapels; the stellar vaulting is adorned with carved bosses; the capitals and bases of the pier shafts are wreathed in sculptured flowers and foliage, and the exterior is enriched with canopied niches once filled with statues. This hardly accords with St Bernard's denunciation of the luxuries in which monks of other Orders indulged, his passionate condemnation 'of the immense height of their Churches, of their immoderate length, of their superfluous breadth, costly polishing and strange designs, which while they attract the eye of the worshipper, hinder the soul's devotion'. Melrose still, however, reveals its Cistercian origin in the shortness of its eastern limb and in the characteristic arrangement of the buildings round the cloister garth, where the sacristy instead of the monks' parlour is immediately next to the church, the frater at right angles to the cloister, and the kitchen within the cloister proper, instead of outside it, as in Benedictine and Cluniac foundations. All this is apparent in the complete ground plan of the abbey uncovered by excavations carried out in 1921. The cloister at Melrose lies to the north instead of to the south of the church as was more usual. This was probably because of the position of the abbey in relation to the Tweed and the advantage of being able to use the river for drainage.

After Robert Bruce had secured the independence of the country at Bannockburn in 1314, architectural inspiration in Scotland was drawn largely from France, and French influence is evident at Melrose in the south transept and also in the east window with its remains of flamboyant tacery and extremely slender shafts. No fewer than five master masons are said to have worked at Melrose. The one among them who is commemorated by a tablet in the south transept, John Moreau, is thought to have been responsible for the east window, and from his name may actually have been French.

49 JEDBURGH ABBEY, ROXBURGHSHIRE. THE SOUTH AISLE AND NAVE

Like Melrose, Jedburgh was founded by David I. It was initially, in c. 1138, a priory of Augustinian canons, brought by John, Bishop of Glasgow, from the Abbey St Quentin, Beauvais, to this site in the narrow valley of the Jed. The monastery became an abbey in 1147. The distinction was that as a priory Jedburgh had been a branch of the abbey at Beauvais, and was presided over by a prior who was subordinate to the abbot of St Quentin; as an abbey it was under the rule of an independent abbot, the prior becoming the second in command, responsible for the discipline of the house. The canons, although they lived according to rule, had more freedom than the regular monks and were allowed to serve in the appropriated churches placed under them.

Jedburgh was repeatedly plundered by the English and was reduced to a state of ruin by the Earl of Hertford in 1545. At the Reformation in 1560 it was acquired by the Kers of Ferniehurst and from this time until 1875 the west end of the nave, the only part of the building to survive entire, was used as a parish church.

The nave is a splendid work of the transitional period; the pointed arches of the arcade and clerestory contrast with the round containing arches of the triforium, while the Early English foliated capitals of the clerestory shafts are entirely different in feeling from the bell-capped clustered shafts from which the triforium arches spring and from the simple square plinths of the main piers, which are distinctly Norman in form. The wild Border life under which Jedburgh so greatly suffered is commemorated in the phrase 'Jeddart justice', which denotes the practice of hanging the criminal first and trying him afterwards.

50 ST ABB'S, BERWICKSHIRE

The village of St Abb's with its neat row of identical, dormered, one-storeyed cottages confronting kitchens and wash-houses (probably the original dwellings) across the road, contrasts with its site near the wild Berwickshire coast and the lofty cape known as St Abb's Head, named after Abb or Ebba, daughter of the Northumbrian King Ethelfrid, foundress of the monastery of *Urbs Coludi* or Coldingham near by. The cottages are constructed of stone, the outbuildings are weatherboarded, the boards being used vertically in the Scandinavian and Dutch style, whereas in the south of Britain horizontal boarding is the rule. The roofs of these outbuildings were probably all formerly made of pantiles, which still cover two of them. This form of roofing, originally introduced from Holland during the 17th century, enjoyed considerable popularity in places on or near the north-east coast of Britain from the East Riding northwards through Berwick and on into Scotland throughout the 18th and much of the 19th century. The fishing inhabitants of St Abb's are said to have been largely Dutch at one time and this may account for the preference for pantiles. The cottages themselves are slated, since pantiles, owing to their large size and wavy line are best used for roofs of the simplest shape and can only with difficulty be adapted to dormers.

51 NEWHAVEN, MIDLOTHIAN. THE HARBOUR

Although it adjoins Edinburgh, Newhaven is still a place of strong individual character. The population, like that of St Abb's, originally came largely from Holland. Newhaven fishwives can still very occasionally be seen in the streets of Edinburgh wearing the voluminous skirts of their traditional dress, though the characteristic stripes are seldom now in evidence. The distant coast seen from the harbour across the Firth of Forth is that of Fife.

52 FOUNTAINHALL, EAST LOTHIAN

In its ancient walled garden, surrounded by densely wooded country, Fountainhall is one of the most romantic of the smaller fortified houses of the Lowlands. It dates chiefly from the 16th and 17th centuries and has hardly been altered since 1638. The original house was probably a free-standing tower of an earlier date than the 16th century. It may have been developed later as were certain tower houses in England, such as Belsay, by the addition of wings; or as in the case of Broughton Castle, by the addition of a hall house. The present aspect of Fountainhall recalls that of Jigginstown Castle in Ireland, an immensely long building with wings. The wings here take the form of a cross-block to the east, as in the plan of a traditional hall house, and a west wing with its roof parallel to that of the main block. The long north face shown in the photograph is interrupted only by the circular stair-tower, in the foot of which is a gun-loop protecting the door just east of it. It is clear that the eastern cross-block with its picturesque outside stair was the latest addition to the house, for a dormer pediment bears the date 1638 and the initials J. P. and M. D. for John Pringle and his wife Margaret Dickson.

If the exterior of the house shows some affinities with developed hall-house designs in the south, the interior conforms to the usual tower-house arrangement with the ground floor given up to storage and domestic offices and the first floor occupied by the principal rooms with sleeping accommodation above them. In the time of the Pringles the house was appropriately called Woodhead. The name Fountainhall was given to it by Sir John Lauder, who bought the property in 1681. Another name by which it is known is Penkaet Castle.

53 THE HOUSE OF THE BINNS, WEST LOTHIAN
The Binns, named after two low hills on the western slope of which it stands, began as a fortified house. It was so much altered at a later date, however, that it now looks like a typical monument of the Picturesque movement, essentially horizontal in feeling though adorned with such medieval trappings as corbelling, battlements, and turrets. The peacock and luxuriant vegetation encourage this impression and create a mellow, dream-like atmosphere in which the question of time and locality seems for the moment irrelevant. The battlements, so placed as to emphasise the horizontal lines of the façades, were indeed the work of the early 19th century; they were introduced in 1810 by the architect William Burn to replace a series of irregular, crow-stepping and pointed turrets and to pull the design together. The south side of the house, shown in the photograph, the site of the earlier courtyard, assumed its present appearance in 1745. It was then that the long windows lighting the dining-room and morning-room were inserted and the pedimented dormers added. The decorations of the interior of the house include some remarkable 17th-century plaster ceilings, especially in the so-called King's Room with its deeply moulded frieze of pomegranates and other fruit, medallions of King David and King Alexander, and robust Royal Arms over the mantelpiece. The craftsman was probably Alexander White.

The Binns was acquired by Thomas Dalyell or Dalzell in 1612 and has remained in the hands of his descendants ever since.

The house figures in many legends, most of which centre about the vivid personality of Thomas Dalzell's son, General Tam Dalzell. He signed the Covenant of 1637, but when it came to the point found himself unable to be disloyal to Charles I. He had early adopted a military career, served in Ireland, then joined the army raised to invade England when Charles II was crowned in Scotland, and was taken prisoner by Cromwell and thrown into the Tower. He escaped, fled to the Continent and entered the service of Czar Alexis Michaelovitch. After the Restoration the General returned to Scotland and was charged with the suppression of the Covenanters whom he defeated at Rullion Green. After this event he was commonly referred to as the 'Bluidie Muscovite'. Nevertheless he was so angered when the women and children to whom he had given quarter at Rullion Green were later shot in Edinburgh, that he resigned his commission and retired to the Binns, where he spent the next ten years planting and developing his estate. In 1679 Charles II appointed him Commander-in-Chief of the Forces in Scotland. He organised a new regiment which held its first muster at the Binns and became famous as the Royal Scots Greys. General Tam was appointed a member of the Privy Council in 1667 and attended his last meeting on 20th August, 1685, the day before he died.

The General, mounted on a white charger, is said to have been often seen on moonlit nights riding up to the house from the ruined bridge over the Errack Burn; and there is a story that he once beat the Devil at cards and that his infernal opponent hurled the card table at Tam's head in a fit of rage. It missed him and fell into the pond used to water the horses of the Greys. Perhaps the tale was not all fantasy, for in the abnormally dry summer of 1878 a heavy table of carved marble was recovered from the mud at the bottom of the pond, where it had lain for two hundred years.

54 ROSSLYN CHAPEL, MIDLOTHIAN

If the serenity and low lines of the Binns strike an unusual note in a countryside which is scenically spectacular and architecturally dramatically vertical, the extraordinary interior of Rosslyn Chapel is yet more unexpected, and dazzles the eye and perplexes the mind with its altogether alien exuberance. Spanish and Portuguese influence determined its strange character, and the chapel is reminiscent in much of its exotic detail of the church of Belem near Lisbon, while the decorative motifs of the transom seen on the left of the photograph are almost identical with those on the richly ornamented Infante's Tomb at Miraflores in Spain. The fantastic pillar in the foreground, with its spirals of flowers and foliage, recalls those in the court of the College of S. Gregorio, Valladolid. The imagery of its base, too, is redolent of the south of Europe where the bodies of just such reptiles, lizards, and scaly dragons so often writhe under the weight of massive pillars, symbols of demons subdued by the power of the Church. The column takes its name, the Prentice Pillar, from a familiar story that it was carved by an apprentice who was slain by his master in a fit of jealousy. The chapel is the choir of a church of which the nave was never built. It was founded as a collegiate church in 1446 by William Sinclair, third Earl of Orkney.

55 BORTHWICK CASTLE, MIDLOTHIAN

The photograph vividly conveys the startling effect of this massively austere fortalice when it first comes into sight on the Galashiels road. This effect it owes in part at least to the remarkable state of preservation of the castle, which is entire except for the loss of its corbelled parapet on the east wall of the main block, while neither crumbling masonry nor rambling ivy softens the overwhelming power of the stark design. Set in a lonely valley, Borthwick is protected on three sides by the Gore and North Middleton Waters, while on the south it was originally guarded by curtain walls and flanking towers. One of these remains and serves as a gatehouse. As a tower-house design Borthwick is of great interest. Two huge towers project to the west from the main block, the space between them proportionally so narrow that it is like a deep, dark chasm. This unusual arrangement enables the medieval hall-house plan to be carried out both vertically and horizontally, for the first floor contains kitchen, great hall and solar in the sequence they occupy in the traditional hall house; at the same time the vaulted chamber below the hall is used for storage, and above it is a private chamber and oratory, thus constituting an up-ended hall house. This dominant theme of the interior is elaborated by numerous wall chambers, stairways and garderobes and by different floor levels.

The castle was built by the first Lord Borthwick c. 1430 and is still owned by the Borthwick family. Mary Queen of Scots and Bothwell were alarmed here a month after their marriage by the confederate Lords and fled to Cakemuir Castle, Mary disguised as a page.

56 CRICHTON CASTLE, MIDLOTHIAN

Like Caerlaverock, these majestic ruins combine a medieval tower house with later additions in a more domestic style. They stand grandly on a projecting point above a glen through the depths of which Tyne Water runs. The tall narrow tower with corbelled parapet, which was the original castle, was built in the 15th century by Chancellor Sir William Crichton who, with the Earl of Callander, was joint guardian of James II during his minority. During the life of the Chancellor the castle was besieged, taken, and almost destroyed by William Earl of Douglas. In the reign of James IV it became the property of the Hepburns (Lord Bothwell) and was rebuilt during the 16th and 17th centuries. Some of the later work is in striking contrast to the vernacular character of the older portions of the fortress. The north side of the courtyard, for intance, completed in 1585, is arcaded and rusticated in the Italian manner.

57 TANTALLON CASTLE, EAST LOTHIAN

Once a stronghold of the Douglases and proverbially impregnable, Tantallon is built on a high rock overhanging the sea which surrounds it on three sides. The only approach is from the west, where it was once protected by a double moat. It was taken by James IV in 1527 but only through the treachery of one of the defenders. In the 17th century, the Marquis of Douglas being a loyal supporter of Charles I, it was wrecked by the Covenanters under General Monk. The castle dates from the 14th century, and departs from the usual arrangement of the tower house enclosed by the barmkin in that the main tower is part of the heavily fortified western entrance with the courtyard behind it. The photograph shows the crude character of the masonry and the thickness of the walls. The material is a carboniferous limestone. This is the interior of the tower and the roughly fashioned openings on the right were fireplaces.

58 THE AULD BRIG, ALLOWAY, AYRSHIRE

Robert Burns was born at Alloway in 1759 in a cottage which combines an authentic period setting with sentimental associations and is now part of the adjacent museum of Burns relics. The simple stone bridge over the Doon and the bosky slopes by the river still preserve something of the atmosphere of the scenes which inspired the well-known lines:

> Aft hae I roved by bonnie Doon
> To see the woodbine twine,
> And ilka bird sang o' its love;
> And sae did I o' mine.

Through the arch can be seen the Burns Monument designed by Thomas Hamilton in 1820, a replica of the circular, classical temple which commemorates the poet on Calton Hill, Edinburgh (see pl. 8). It contains more Burns relics, including the wedding ring of his wife, Jean Armour.

59 BURNS MONUMENT, ALLOWAY, AYRSHIRE

The creator of this unforgettable work was a local sculptor, James Thom, who towards the end of his life in 1850 made a name for himself in New York, where his outrageous realism entertains the visitor to Trinity Church. Another powerful example of his unique art can be seen at Ayr where a statue of the national hero looks down from a niche in the Wallace Tower. But Thom's masterpiece must surely be these two seated figures, placed in a grotto close to the monument shown on the opposite page. The vigour of the execution and the meticulous realism allied to a spirit more often found in the popular than the sophisticated arts makes this a more fitting memorial to the poet than the Corinthian temple. The figures are life-size, carved in red sandstone, and the

133

sculptor's faithful rendering in so unlikely a material of the diverse textures of wood, flesh, and fabric, of even the variations occasioned by the use of different stitches in knitting, leaves the spectator dumbfounded. The sculptures represent two characters from *Tam o' Shanter,* Tam himself and Souter Johnnie.

60 AILSA CRAIG, AYRSHIRE

This view of the islet of Ailsa Craig at sunset, its precipitous granite cliffs and fissured, irregular outline smoothed by distance and the level light into a simple dome shape, perfectly conveys the atmosphere of the Ayrshire coast which, rocky, wooded and deeply romantic, is steeped in a softness combined with an intensity of colour more often associated with Ireland than with Scotland.

61 DUNURE CASTLE, AYRSHIRE

These fragmentary remains of a former tower house of the Kennedy family crown a promontory above the sea. The beehive-shaped structure so remarkably silhouetted against the sky, water and the distant outline of the Isle of Arran, is an ancient dovecot. With its bell-like curves and dry-stone walling it looks as though it may have been constructed from a former broch (*see* pl. VI and 122).

62 CULZEAN CASTLE, AYRSHIRE

Robert Adam worked almost exclusively in the classical style, but he was nevertheless not unaffected by the taste for the Picturesque which reached its height during his life-time. One of the most frequently recurring images in his landscape sketches is a half-ruined medieval castle; the architect he most admired, Vanbrugh, was anti-classical in his creation of a style of dramatic chiaroscuro, colossal scale and movement; and Adam himself stressed the importance of the essentially 'picturesque' quality of movement in his design for the south front of Kedleston. It is also worth recalling that Robert's father, William Adam, had presented him with a ruined castle at Dowhill, close to the Blair Adam estate in Kinross-shire, and that this may have stimulated an interest in the style which he used so effectively for his romantic designs for Culzean and Lauder Castles. Only the former was carried out and it was built between 1771 and 1792 for the tenth Earl of Cassilis, the chief of the Kennedys, to incorporate an ancient tower house which had already been enlarged before Adam started work. The castle is a typical product of the 18th-century Picturesque style, a building of Georgian symmetry and order with medieval trimmings. Swelling towers and turrets, battlements and machicolations are combined with sash windows and Adam's characteristic arched recesses in the Palladian tradition. The principal idea of the building is of a great circular tower rising abruptly from the cliff edge and projecting from the main pile, a central block with wings.

The interior of Culzean is entirely classical and in the style for which Adam is famous, the seaward tower and the angle turrets providing that variety in the shape of the rooms which Adam particularly encouraged. The Round Drawing Room which fills the first floor of the tower, thus occupying the place of the great hall in the traditional tower house, and commanding a magnificent view over the Firth of Clyde, shows Adam at his best. Every detail—tables, chandeliers, girandoles, even the door-handles—was designed by the architect; the carpet was woven to his design at the local town of Maybole and his drawing for the ceiling is preserved in the castle.

The house was known as The Cove until the end of the 17th century, although a grandson of the first owner of the castle, John Kennedy, signed himself 'Joannes Kennedy de Culzane' in 1492. Adam's patron wrote it 'Cullean' and in the parish records the house is referred to as 'Covelean'.

63 THE FORTH BRIDGE, MIDLOTHIAN

The Forth Bridge, 2,765½ yards long and 361 feet above the water, was one of the great engineering feats of the 19th century. It was built to the design of Sir John Fowler, assisted by Sir Benjamin Baker in 1863–90, on the cantilever system with two main spans of 1710 feet each and two smaller side spans of 689¾ feet each. When the work was at its height 5,000 men were employed; and 54,000 tons of steel were used in the construction. The photograph, taken from the air, gives some idea of the impressive effect and stupendous scale of this graceful structure flung into the vast panorama across the shining expanse of water like a string of giant, elliptical openwork beads. The Bridge is used exclusively for railway traffic, while its rival, the New Forth Bridge, seen on the left, built between 1958 and 1965, is for road traffic.

64 THE NEW FORTH BRIDGE, MIDLOTHIAN

The photograph, taken from the slipway of the ferry, illustrates the contrast between the two huge engineering works, the one swelling and contracting and boldly patterned by the criss-cross of its gargantuan girders, the other a simple horizontal design, varied only by the verticals of the piers and the airy curves of the cables. The new structure is a suspension bridge with the incredible span of 3,300 feet between the main piers, each of which towers up to a height of 512 feet. It is the largest suspension bridge in Europe; and like the old bridge it captures the imagination both as a staggering engineering feat and as a visual image. In both cases a purely functional work becomes a satisfying design because of the appropriately tremendous scale of the geometric repeating units.

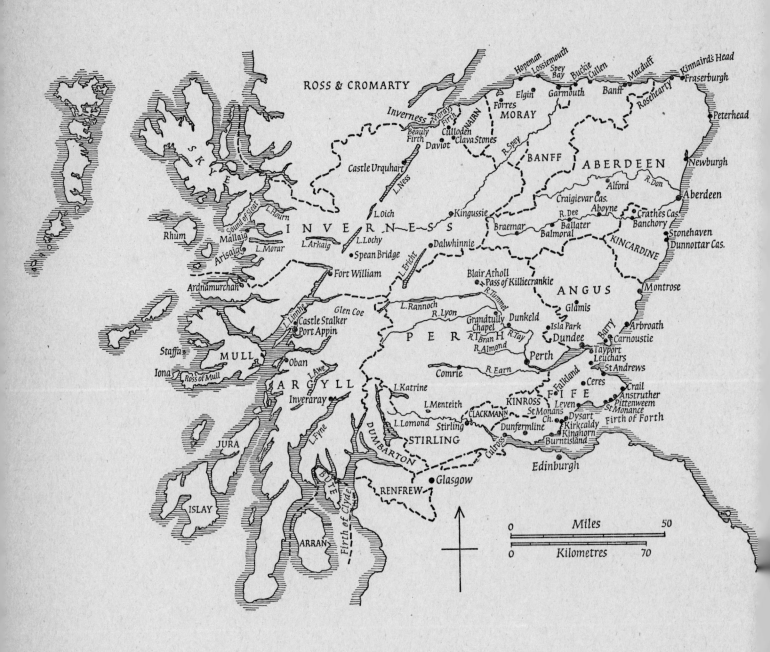

Part Three CENTRAL SCOTLAND

ROSS & CROMARTY

SKYE

Inverness
Moray Firth
NAIRN
Forres
MORAY
Elgin
Hopeman
Lossiemouth
Spey Bay
Buckie
Cullen
Macduff
Kinnaird's Head
Fraserburgh
Rosehearty
Banff
Garmouth
Peterhead

Beauly Firth
Culloden
Clava Stones
Daviot
R. Spey
BANFF
ABERDEEN
Newburgh

Castle Urquhart
L. Ness

Alford
R. Don
Craigievar Cas.
Aboyne
Crathes Cas.
Aberdeen
Kingussie
R. Dee
Banchory
Braemar
Ballater
Stonehaven
Balmoral
KINCARDINE
Dunnottar Cas.

L. Oich
Dalwhinnie

INVERNESS
L. Lochy
L. Arkaig
Spean Bridge
L. Ericht
Blair Atholl
Pass of Killiecrankie
ANGUS
Montrose

Rhum
Mallaig
L. Morar
L. Hourn
Sound of Sleat

Arisaig

Fort William
Glamis

Ardnamurchan
L. Rannoch
R. Lyon
R. Tummel
Grandtully
Chapel
Dunkeld
Isla Park
Arbroath
Dundee
Carnoustie
Barry

Glen Coe
Linnhe
Castle Stalker
Port Appin
PERTH
R. Tay
R. Bran
R. Almond
Tayport
Leuchars
St Andrews

Staffa
MULL
Oban
L. Awe
Comrie
R. Earn
Perth
Falkland
Ceres
Crail

Iona
Ross of Mull
ARGYLL
Inveraray
L. Katrine
FIFE
Anstruther
Pittenweem
St Monance

L. Menteith
KINROSS
Leven
St Monans
Ch.
Dysart
JURA
L. Fyne
L. Lomond
CLACKMANN
Stirling
Dunfermline
Kirkcaldy
Kinghorn
Burntisland
Firth of Forth

DUMBARTON
STIRLING
Culross
Edinburgh

BUTE
Glasgow
RENFREW

ISLAY

ARRAN
Firth of Clyde

0   Miles   50

0   Kilometres   70

66

67

68

69

71

72

93

94

96

97

101

65 DUNKELD CATHEDRAL, PERTHSHIRE. WINDOW IN THE SOUTH NAVE WALL

The photograph shows the flamboyant tracery, in the French style, for which the aisle windows of Dunkeld are famous. Through the window can be seen the curious semi-circular openings of the clerestory which were very popular in Scotland during the latter half of the 15th century. The nave was in fact consecrated by Bishop Lauder in 1464. Later in the 15th century Gavin Douglas became Dunkeld's most distinguished bishop; he was a poet celebrated for his spirited translation of the *Aeneid*. The choir, now used as the parish church, was built a century earlier and was restored in 1600 after the whole building had been wrecked by the Reformers in 1560. In their fanatical zeal they far exceeded their orders which, respecting this building, ran: 'Faill not, bot ze tak guid heyd that neither the dasks, windocks, nor duires, be ony ways hurt or broken—eyther glassin wark or iron wark.' It was the end of the bishopric which had endured since the time of Alexander I (1107–24). The east end of the cathedral was again extensively restored during the 19th century, chiefly at the expense of the Duke of Atholl, and yet once more in 1908; thus, although it is full of interesting monu-ments, its fabric is no longer medieval. The ruined nave, on the other hand, is one of the most noble and evocative of all Scotland's ecclesiastical remains. The architectural forms, worn, smoothed, and attenuated, and blotched with lichen, are like natural growths, completely at one with the magnificent surrounding landscape.

The venerable building stands on a shaven lawn beside the broad, sparkling, swift-flowing Tay, just to the left of the main street of the charming little white-washed town. Looking toward the cathedral from the elegant seven-arched bridge designed by Telford in 1809, the spectator sees the great tower rising against a richly wooded valley surrounded by mountains, not so lofty as those of the central and western Highlands, of which they are the outliers, but adding just that degree of grandeur and irregularity to the scene which attracted Picturesque travellers of the late 18th century.

66 ARCHBISHOP SHARP'S BRIDGE, CERES, FIFESHIRE

This small, half ruinous village by the Eden above the wooded glen of Dura Den is
not named after the Roman goddess but after St Cyr. The place has a dreamlike
atmosphere, rather rare in the bracing climate of Scotland's east coast. The vegetation
is unusually luxuriant, especially along the banks of the stream, and there is a peculiar
magic about the houses, clustered near a green, quiet, neglected and sometimes decorated with robustly sculptured heraldic devices by a local 17th-century artist. The present
sense of peace scarcely harmonises with the events commemorated by the name of the
bridge. Archbishop Sharp passed across it on the night of 3rd May, 1679, shortly
before he was waylaid and murdered by a party of Covenanters.

67 CRAIL, FIFESHIRE

The fishermen of Crail are largely 'inshore', that is to say, they fish near the coast and
land their catches daily, using small open boats like the one in the photograph. The
charming group of vernacular buildings with their crow-stepped gables and pantiles
(see pl. 50), is seen to advantage behind its picturesque foreground of cobbles and
creels. The equipment shows the extent to which creel fishing for lobsters and crabs is
carried on here. Behind the cottages runs the stone wall of a Victorian mansion with
a castellated gazebo overlooking the sea. The parish church was a collegiate foundation
of 1517. In 1559 John Knox preached a sermon here against the monuments of
idolatry which so inflamed his audience that they set off at once for St Andrews, a
few miles away, and destroyed its cathedral.

68 DYSART, FIFESHIRE

An old seaport dominated by the fortress-like tower of the ruined church of St Serf,
a hermit saint of the 5th century. The corbelled parapet of the tower, the crow-stepped
gables of some of the houses, and the combination of stone, pantile and harling are all
eloquent of the locality of Dysart.

69 ST MONANS CHURCH, ST MONANCE, FIFESHIRE

The church, built in c. 1362 by David II, in gratitude for having been healed of a
wound at the saint's shrine, was planned as a cruciform building, which was never
completed. The present church consists of the chancel and transepts of the original
plan together with the squat tower over the crossing surmounted by the short steeple
with spire lights which is the most characteristic form of tower in medieval parish
churches in Scotland. With no adornment apart from its window tracery and gable-
topped angle buttresses, the church is dramatically massed on the very edge of the sea

in a westward-sloping graveyard here striped with the long afternoon shadows of obelisks and urn-crowned pedestals.

The interior of St Monans was until a year or two ago one of the most moving not only in Scotland but in all Britain. Although the actual date of the church is 14th-century, the tower arches are Early English in feeling, with lancet points, even though the shafts with their plainly moulded capitals are engaged instead of detached. The simple and beautiful ribbed vault is wholly Early English in character. This impressive stonework survives unaltered. But it was the furniture in this noble setting which gave St Monans its special atmosphere. The church has always served a fishing community and was decorated with models of fishing smacks and trawlers, while the fine box pews were covered with graffiti representing open boats, deep-sea trawlers, fishing gear and all kinds of fish—plaice, hake and herring clearly recognisable among them. Pews and models have now been swept away to make room for modern pews of aggressively angular design, while between them runs a strip of red carpet made specially for the purpose in the Paisley factory.

70 DUNFERMLINE ABBEY, FIFESHIRE

The nave of Dunfermline Abbey instantly recalls that of Durham, which preceded it by about 25 years. The scale is less grand, there is not the same overwhelming effect of mass occasioned by the immense girth of the pillars and the narrowness of the arcade openings; but again the noble simplicity of the design, and the majestic rhythm of the arcade and the austere triforium with its perfectly plain round arches combined with the bold, unsophisticated decoration of the sturdy, cylindrical piers, grooved with zig-zags and spirals, are indescribably moving. There is a factual as well as a stylistic connection with Durham, for King Malcolm Canmore of Dunfermline was present at the founding of Durham on 11th August, 1093, by Bishop William of St Calais. After the Norman Conquest Malcolm entertained the royal refugees from England at Dunfermline, then the royal burgh, and in 1070 he married one of them—Margaret, sister of Edgar Atheling. Soon after her marriage in 1074 Queen Margaret founded a priory at Dunfermline, which superseded Iona as a place of royal sepulture. Queen Margaret herself and Malcolm are among those who lie buried here; their tombs are in the present churchyard in the place to the east of the church where a Lady Chapel once stood. The monks of the new priory were Benedictines from Canterbury. In 1128 David I, son of Margaret and Malcolm, erected the priory into an abbey, and began a new and more imposing church. It was probably then that the Norman nave was built: the aisled choir and transept were added in the Early English style between 1216 and 1226 under Abbot Patrick, who had formerly been Prior of Canterbury. The monastery, described by a famous contemporary, Matthew Paris, as of such vast extent 'and containing such magnificent palaces that three kings with their trains might be accommodated within its walls', was almost entirely destroyed by the soldiers of Edward I in 1303; the church alone was spared. The reason for this act of destruction, according to Matthew Paris, was that 'the Scots had converted the house of the Lord into a den of thieves, by holding their rebellious Parliaments there'. Some two hundred and fifty years later the church itself fell a victim to the zeal of the Reformers when on 28th March, 1560, 'the whole lordis and barnis that were on this syde of Forth, passed to Stirling, and be the way kest down the Abbey of Dunfermline'. The transepts and east end of the church were laid in ruins; the south-west tower escaped the fury of the Reformers only to be struck by lightning in 1870. The nave and fragments of the refectory and kitchen are all that now survive of the once splendid abbey. A new choir in the Gothic Revival style was built over the remains of the old chancel by William Burn in 1817–22; it has all the lightness and elegance of the same architect's work at St John's Edinburgh (see pl. 19) and enhances by comparison the weight and solemnity of the nave.

71 LEUCHARS CHURCH, FIFESHIRE

It would be difficult to imagine a more unexpected association of architectural styles or a more surprising composition than those exemplified in the amazing parish church of Leuchars. A 17th-century octagonal tower surmounted by a lantern and cupola sits above a richly arcaded Norman semicircular apse against the gable end of a Norman choir, with a taller 17th-century nave tacked on behind it. Both apse and choir are adorned with two tiers of arcading separated by a string course, carved with zigzags, or with scroll floral motifs. The apse arches are flanked by cushion-capped shafts and are themselves ornamented with chevron and billet mouldings, the upper tier with an extra, broad order of billets. The lower arcade of the choir is formed of interlacing arches, probably indicating that this part of the church is of later date than the apse. The cornice of both apse and choir is supported by a series of grotesque corbel heads. The apsidal end is itself an unusual sight to anyone accustomed to the square east end which had become general in England and Wales by the time Leuchars was built in the mid 12th century. But an eastern apse with a classical tower rising immediately over its Romanesque cornice is a wholly exotic image. It is none the less extraordinarily convincing and unified, partly because it is all built in the same grey local stone and time and weather have eliminated the differences in texture between the tower and the apse and choir. The exact date of the early structure is not known. A reference to the 'Ecclesia de Lochres' in the registry of the Priory of St Andrews shows that a building existed in 1187, and Orabile, Countess of Mar recorded that she was present when her father Nes gave the church of Leuchars to the Canons of St Andrews in c. 1171.

72 ELGIN CATHEDRAL, MORAYSHIRE

The photograph shows the south choir aisle of the former cathedral with its groined vault and clustered piers of the late 13th century. The knightly effigy in the foreground is that of Hay of Lochloy who died in 1422. Despite his remoteness from the centres of fashion he is stylishly dressed in the cuirass and wears a slanting 'bawdrick' or sword belt as well as an ornamental horizontal one, all of which were not common before about 1415. The knight's feet rest, as was usual, upon a lion. This choir aisle and the chapter house are the best preserved parts of a cathedral which, like Salisbury, seems to have been remarkable for the consistency of its style. But the tiers of lancet openings of late 13th-century design with which we are now so eloquently confronted belong to the only parts of the cathedral which escaped a fire of 1390, when, after a quarrel with the bishop, the 'Wolf of Badenoch', brother of Robert III, attacked the building. The rest was rebuilt with a central tower, which collapsed in 1506. It was restored in 1538, only to fall again in 1711. In 1555 the interior of the cathedral was desecrated and severely damaged by an outbreak of violence between the Dunbar and Innes families, whose names are commemorated by the transepts, known as the Innes and Dunbar Aisles. In 1567 the roof was stripped of its lead, supposedly to raise funds to pay the troops fighting under the Earl of Moray against Mary. In the following century Cromwell's men tore down the wood loft and smashed the west window.

The choir is six bays in length, thus of exactly the same proportion as the nave, which has vanished except for some fragments of piers. This relationship accords with English practice and with the design of other cathedrals in Scotland, such as Dunblane and St Andrews, but is quite unlike that of most conventual churches in Scotland, where the choir is short by comparison with the nave.

73 LOCH LOMOND, DUNBARTONSHIRE

'Everything here is romantic beyond description. This country is justly styled the Arcadia of Scotland, and I don't doubt but that it may vie with Arcadia in everything but climate. I am sure that it excels it in verdure, wood, and water. What say you to a natural bason of pure water, nearly thirty miles long, and in some places seven miles broad, and in many above an hundred fathoms deep, having four and twenty habitable islands, some of them stocked with deer and all of them covered with wood; containing immense quantities of delicious fish, salmon, pike, trout, perch, flounders, eels, and powans, the last a delicate kind of fresh-water herring peculiar to this lake; and finally, communicating with the sea, by sending off the Leven, through which all those species (except the powan) make their exit and entrance occasionally!'

This was Smollett's description of Loch Lomond in *Humphry Clinker*. It was part of the landscape of his childhood, for he was born on the banks of the Leven at

Dalguharn House. The scene is no longer as Smollett knew it, for the inevitable accompaniment of modern tourism, heavy traffic along the narrow road, has sullied the west shore of the loch with litter, ruined the character of the villages and shattered the solitude essential to the experience of the romantic and the sublime. Yet at certain seasons and at certain times of day it is still possible to be overwhelmed by the grandeur of this immense sheet of water. It is seen here from its northern end in a burst of dazzling light on a stormy day. It is shaded on the left by Ben Lomond and in the far distance, almost transparent in the luminous atmosphere, a shoal of islands closes the shining vista. The lake was anciently called Loch Leven, and gave its name to the surrounding country, which became known as Levenax or Lennox. The principal clans living on the shores of the loch were the MacGregors and the Colquhouns, who engaged in deadly combat in Glen Fruin at the south-west end of the lake in 1603. Two hundred of the Colquhouns were killed and a number of outsiders, who had been shut up in a barn for safety, were murdered in cold blood by the MacGregors. One of their clan was the celebrated freebooter, Rob Roy or Robert Rua MacGregor, with whom the whole district is associated.

74 INVERARAY CASTLE, ARGYLLSHIRE

The view from the classical bridge across the Aray, of the castle on its snow-covered bank, with the jagged, wintry heights of the mountains of Glen Orchy behind it, captures the essence of all that Scotland suggests to the romantic imagination: the grandeur of nature, the fantastic character of the architecture and the richness of its historical associations. The wildness of the country beyond the castle grounds was forcibly conveyed when the photograph was being taken by a huge peregrine falcon swooping through the clear, icy air, with a rushing sound like the noise of a rocket, to alight on the balustrade, there to perch with its head sunk into its shoulders, and its breast turned outward, absolutely motionless, all its fierce, alien life confined to its glittering eye. As for the castle, not only is its square, turreted shape, with a massive battlemented tower rising from its heart, utterly unexpected and exotic, especially if the pretty, gothic windows of the central tower are glimpsed above the roof-line, but its strange colour gives it a mysterious air of unreality. It is built of blue-green granite, and the cones of its slated angle-towers are stained a deeper green by the actions of the weather. It is as though the hue of the fabric had been mixed from the greens of the setting—of the dark, polished foliage of evergreens, the matt, limy moss on tree trunks and the bottle-glass sheen of the river. With regard to associations, the history of the castle is bound up with that of the Campbells, Dukes of Argyll, two of whom were beheaded, one as leader of the Covenanters, the other as an ardent supporter of Monmouth.

The castle replaces a 15th-century stronghold and was built in 1746 for the Third Duke by Roger Morris and William Adam. It is thus a very early work of the Gothic Revival, for it was only in 1747 that Horace Walpole acquired the farm at Twickenham which was to become Strawberry Hill, the starting point for standard accounts of the style. Roger Morris was the author of several books on architecture, among which were *Rural Architecture* (1750) and *Architecture Improved* (1755), and was essentially a designer in the classical style. He was the author of the Palladian bridge at Wilton and of the centre block of the White House, Richmond Park. Inveraray Castle, in common with other Gothic works of the Georgian period, including Culzean Castle (pl. 62), is basically a symmetrical, classical composition to which medieval and Picturesque details have been added. In a Palladian house of the time the centrally placed hall would probably have taken the form of a dome; it is the castellated outline of this feature and its size in relation to the rest of the building which give Inveraray so eccentric an air. This tower must have dominated the house to a still greater degree before the attic storey was added to the main building after a fire in 1877. It was at this time that the angle turrets were furnished with the conical caps which now seem so inevitable a part of the composition.

75 INVERARAY CASTLE, ARGYLLSHIRE. THE CENTRAL HALL
The hall dates from 1877 when the castle was restored after the fire mentioned in the previous note. It is one of the most impressive interiors of the late 19th century, the decorative detail of the lofty apartment consisting almost exclusively in the brilliantly original display of weapons, swords, pikes, halberds and rifles, filling the semicircular heads of doors and niches and patterning the overmantel in the form of a giant sun.

76 INVERARAY CASTLE. THE DINING ROOM
The Georgian rooms at Inveraray belong to the late 18th century, to almost the same period as Adam's work at Culzean (pl. 62). They are less well-known than any of Adam's interiors, yet they are among the most enchanting creations of the period. The designer was Robert Mylne, a Scottish architect and engineer, who was described by one who knew him as a man of 'austere manners, violent temper, and contempt for every art except his own and for every person but himself'. The charm and elegance of this dining room almost justify the architect's estimate of his own achievements. Although the decoration is closely related to Adam in style, the proportions and detail show subtle differences. There is a greater naturalism, for instance, in the treatment of the swags against their cloudy background which immediately introduces a feeling of more warmth and spontaneity than is ever found in an Adam apartment. Biagio

Rebecca, who worked also for Adam, was responsible for carrying out this painted ornament, including the illusionist bas-reliefs, for which he had a remarkable gift.

77 LOCH FYNE, ARGYLLSHIRE
Inveraray Castle and the little town in their magnificent setting on the shore of Loch Fyne are here seen from Duniquoich, a hill with a watch tower immediately above the castle grounds. Loch Fyne is a sea loch celebrated for its herring fishing.

78 INVERARAY, ARGYLLSHIRE. THE MAIN STREET
Except for the prominent chimney-stacks, this broad street vista of flat, white façades, closed by a temple-like church, might be Italian. This impression has been strengthened by the removal during the Second World War of the octagonal lantern and tall, thin spire which originally sat on the church roof above the pediment. Inveraray was a planned town, laid out by Robert Mylne for the Third Duke of Argyll at the time when the architect was working on the interior of the castle. The three-storeyed terrace houses are quite different from the traditional one-storeyed cottages of rural Scotland and different again, in their severity, unrelieved by a single pilastered or pedimented doorway, from English terraces of the period. Though no larger than a village, Inveraray is entirely urban and formal in character. It replaced a squalid little town which once clustered about the old castle and which still existed when Smollett wrote *Humphry Clinker*. He mentions the wretched cabins in which the Duke's tenants were living.

79 INVERARAY, ARGYLLSHIRE
A view from the southern portico of the church of the sloping street at right angles to the one shown on the left. There was a reason for the porticos on the north and south of the church: they symbolised the double purpose to which the building was originally put. It was divided inside into two sections, one for services in English for the Duke of Argyll and his household, the other for services in Gaelic for the townspeople.

80 BLAIR CASTLE, PERTHSHIRE
With its harled and whitewashed walls, its corbelled turrets and crow-stepped gables combined unexpectedly with a square tower crowned by heavily corbelled battlements, Blair Castle is typical both of the development of the Scottish tower house in a period when old defensive forms had become mere ornament and French influence was strong, and of the later Scottish Baronial style. The original fortress stood on the site of that part of the building which is nearest to the spectator in the photograph. It was built

by John Comyn in the second half of the 13th century. This early building, of which little can now survive, was enlarged and altered by successive generations of the Earls of Atholl and of the Strathbogie, Stewart, and Murray families. The square tower was probably a 15th-century addition, and a hall range is said to have been added in 1530. Blair was damaged by Cromwell, and in 1745 it was Lord George Murray's painful duty to besiege and bombard his own home, which was occupied by Government troops. In the restoration that followed, Blair Castle underwent an extraordinary transformation. In an attempt to follow the fashion of the day the two upper storeys were removed complete with turrets, battlements, and gables. And when Queen Victoria visited Blair in 1844 she was confronted by 'a large, plain, white building' no longer known as Blair Castle but called Atholl House. However, the Queen's enthusiasm for Scotland and the Scottish vernacular style brought another change. David Bryce, the well-known 'Scottish Baronial' architect, was asked by the Duke to restore the vanished turrets, crow-steps, and battlements. The projecting portion of the façade immediately beyond the square tower replaces the Georgian entrance of Atholl House and is entirely Victorian; the rest of the house is a mixture of authentic and 19th-century masonry and detail. Blair Castle dominates the Strath of Atholl above the wooded Pass of Killiecrankie. The term *strath*, as opposed to *glen*, a steep, narrow defile, signifies a broad, cultivated valley.

81 GLENCOE, ARGYLLSHIRE

This photograph was taken from the road near the so-called Study (a corruption of the Scots 'stiddie', meaning anvil) and the head of the gorge with the peak of Stob Coire nan Lochan rising behind Beinn Fhada, Gedrr Aonach, and Aonach Dubh, the so-called three sisters of Glencoe. The viewpoint is almost the same as that chosen by Horatio MacCulloch in 1864 when he painted the picture of the glen now in the Glasgow Art Gallery. It was also the spot where Queen Victoria elected to picnic when she visited Glencoe in 1873. In the precipitous west face of Aonach Dubh is the narrow cleft of Ossian's Cave above Loch Achtriochtan, where the bard is supposed to have been born. In the poems purporting to be translations from the Gaelic of Ossian, with which James Macpherson took the literary world by storm in 1760, the savage landscape of Glencoe and the waters of the Loch and the Coe, called Cona in the poems, furnish a good deal of the imagery: 'Their sound was like a thousand streams that meet in Cona's vale, when, after a stormy night, they turn their dark eddies beneath the pale light of morning.' 'Why bends the bard of Cona, said Fingal, over his secret stream? Is this a time for sorrow, father of low-laid Oscar?' The Ossian cult, the tragic, historic associations of Glencoe and the eloquent descriptions of earlier travellers, among them the Wordsworths, Macaulay, and Dickens, have all conspired to intensify the sombre aspect of the scene, and neither the construction of a new and easier road in the present century nor the popularity of the glen with tourists and climbers have lessened the stern and menacing effect of the black, curiously naked and jagged rocks.

The setting added to the horror of the massacre which took place there on 13th February, 1692. The Highland chiefs had been asked to swear an oath of allegiance to William of Orange by 31st December, 1691. MacDonald of Glencoe was the last of all to make his submission, partly because, in common with the other chiefs, he wished to obtain the consent of King James to the relinquishing of his allegiance. He presented himself to Colonel Hill, the governor of Fort William, on 31st December, only to be told that the oath could be administered by none but a civil magistrate. Armed with a letter from Hill, MacDonald hastened on to Inveraray but, held up by a snowstorm, arrived only on 2nd January, where after yet further delay the oath was administered and a certificate of MacDonald's submission sent to Edinburgh, so that the case could be referred to the Privy Council. The clerks to the Council, however, decided that a submission made after the prescribed date could not be put before the Council, and though the certificate of submission was accepted, Macdonald's name was deleted.

Meanwhile the Master of Stair, Sir John Dalrymple, Secretary of State, informed Sir Thomas Livingstone, Commander-in-Chief in Scotland, that on the King's instructions military action was to be taken against those chiefs who had not submitted. The Master said that he had just been told that MacDonald of Glencoe had not taken the oath, 'at which I rejoice, it's a great work of charity to be exact in rooting out that damnable sept, the worst in all the Highlands'. In letters written at the end of January to Livingstone and Colonel Hill, Sir John Dalrymple gave more detailed instructions: 'I am glad', he wrote to Livingstone, 'that Glencoe did not come in within the time prescribed. . . . I think to herry their cattle or burn their houses is but to render them desparate lawless men, to rob their neighbours: but I believe you will be satisfied it were a great advantage to the nation that thieving tribe were rooted out and cut off. It must be quietly done, otherwise they will make shift for both the men and their cattle.' In the letter to Hill the Master emphasised the need for secrecy. 'Pray, when anything concerning Glencoe is received, let it be secret and sudden, otherwayes the men will shift you, and better not meddle with them than not to do it to purpose, to cut off that nest of robbers who have fallen in the mercy of law now when their is force and opportunity.'

On Monday, 1st February, one hundred and twenty Campbell soldiers appeared in Glencoe under the command of Captain Robert Campbell of Glenlyon. They were met by John MacDonald, the chief's elder son, to whom they said that, the garrison being overcrowded, they had been ordered to take up their quarters in the glen. The soldiers themselves had not been told the true reason for their presence in Glencoe, the Macdonalds suspected nothing, and the troops were billeted up and down the valley. They were generously entertained and for ten days lived on the best of terms with their hosts. Robert Campbell himself was playing cards with two of MacDonald's sons on the night of 12th February. It is probable that before the game began he had already received instructions to wipe out the whole MacDonald clan on the following morning, 'to fall upon the Rebells, the MacDonalds of Glencoe, and putt all to the sword under seventy, you are to have a speciall care that the old fox and his sones doe upon no account escape your hands, you are to secure all the avenues that no man escape. This you are to putt in executione at fyve of the clock precisely.' The massacre began in the early hours of the morning before it was light. Old MacDonald was shot in the back as he was getting out of bed; a boy of thirteen tried to save himself by clinging to Robert Campbell but was ruthlessly shot down, and a woman and a child of four were among the slain. John MacDonald of Achtriochtan was among the dead. One old man of more than eighty was butchered and another was burned alive in a house where he had taken refuge. Many of the people of the glen escaped to the hills, only to die of exposure and starvation. Yet in spite of their greatly superior numbers and the unexpectedness of their onslaught, the soldiers did not actually kill more than about forty men, and Campbell certainly did not carry out his instructions completely. It is thought that perhaps some of the soldiers, when they realised what they had to do, helped their hosts to escape. Tradition tells of individual troopers trying to warn their hosts. Thus one story relates how a soldier praised his host's plaid, adding that none could tell who would be wearing it on the morrow; and another repeats the words of a soldier spoken aloud to the great stone, 'Clach Eanruig', which still stands in the field beside Carnoch: 'Grey stone of the Glen, though great is thy right to be here, if thou knewest what would happen tonight, thou wouldst no longer tarry here.' Whatever the attitude of the soldiers to this vile act of treachery, the Master of Stair was unmoved and uncontrite. 'All I regret', he said, 'is that any of the sect got away, and there is necessity to persecute them to the utmost.' Colonel Hill, however, who had felt deep disquiet throughout, did his best to secure the resettlement of the MacDonalds in the Glen.

82 THE PASS OF KILLIECRANKIE, PERTHSHIRE

The Pass and the river Garry, hurtling down into a dark pool, are seen from the road between Pitlochry and Kinloch Rannoch. The defile is so narrow that its depths seem to be shrouded in a twilight haze even at noon, and this impression is encouraged by the dense growth of trees which completely covers the abrupt slopes on either side of the stream. The scene appeared so forbidding to a body of Hessian troops, fighting against the Pretender, in the '45, that they refused to march through the pass. It was here in 1689 that the famous battle of Killiecrankie was fought between the Highland troops, commanded by Viscount Dundee, Graham of Claverhouse, and the army of King William, commanded by General Mackay. An upright stone at Urrard House in the woods marks the spot where the noble Dundee fell, fatally wounded, in the moment of victory.

83 DUNNOTTAR CASTLE, KINCARDINESHIRE

For about a mile along the coast at this point the sea is confronted by a formidable natural rampart of pale granite. Upon the very brink of this rampart stand the majestic ruins of Dunnottar Castle, covering an area of nearly three acres and separated from the mainland by a deep chasm. The castle is said to have been built in *c.* 1392 by Sir William Keith, Marischal of Scotland; but a fortress must previously have stood on the site, for there is a record stating that it was taken from the English by William Wallace in 1296. Among the many subsequent additions to the fortress the most significant was the powerful gatehouse of 1575. During the Cromwellian period the Scottish regalia were kept at Dunnottar to preserve them from the Republican army; and a garrison was placed in the castle under the command of Ogilvy of Barras. Besieged by the English under Lambert, the garrison held out with great resolution, though starving, until the regalia had been conveyed away by stratagem and hidden under the pulpit of Kinneff Church. The story goes that Mrs Grainger, wife of the minister of Kinneff, having obtained permission to visit Mrs Ogilvy, the governor's lady, packed up the crown in some clothes, and carried it out of the castle in her lap, while her maid hid the sword and sceptre in a bag of flax slung over her shoulder.

84 CRATHES CASTLE, KINCARDINESHIRE. THE TOWER ROOM

The number of abandoned, decaying tower houses in Scotland is so great that after a time the traveller ceases to respond to the picturesque delights of ruins, and when the disintegration has advanced so far that architectural details are scarcely recognisable, fading pleasure is apt to turn to irritation. To such experiences Crathes, the seat of the ancient family of Burnett of Leys, is a welcome contrast for it has been in continuous occupation since the mid 16th century; and although the castle was twice occupied by Montrose during the Covenanting Wars, the building suffered no damage because of the high esteem in which the laird, Sir Thomas Burnett, was held. The original castle was an L-shaped tower house built between 1553 and 1596, to which a symmetrical and three-storeyed east wing was added at the beginning of the 18th century. The exterior is spectacular, the simple east wing contrasting with the old tower burgeoning into an exuberant array of turrets, dormers, crow-stepped gables, gargoyles, and finials, jutting out from the lofty, harled walls on ornate corbelling.

180

The vaulted Tower Room on the first floor of the 16th-century castle was the original great hall. The present fireplace (a later insertion) occupies the lower end of the hall. At the opposite end there was once a dais where the laird and his family dined. The opening in the corner of the room formerly led to a wall staircase leading to the laird's bedroom above, and to the entrance chamber below. Pendants, bearing the Burnett Arms, three holly leaves and a hunting horn, hang from the vaulted ceiling, and in the case above the fireplace is displayed one of the great treasures of the castle, the bejewelled ivory Horn of Leys. It is reputed to have been given by Robert Bruce to Alexander Burnett, together with the lands of Crathes in 1323. The horn was a badge of office, signifying that Burnett had pledged himself to serve as Coroner of the Royal Forest of Drum in return for the gift of land. The picture to the right of the horn is by George Jamesone, the 17th-century portraitist, no less than five works by whom are preserved at Crathes.

85 CRAIGIEVAR CASTLE, ABERDEENSHIRE. THE HALL
Externally, Craigievar, a 17th-century tower house built in 1610-24, is a splendid example of the way in which Scottish lairds went on building towers on the 14th-century pattern long after the need for them had passed. It rises seven storeys high, like an up-ended matchbox, from a smooth lawn in a landscape of bare rolling hills, crowned by a riot of projecting turrets and high-pitched roofs, the decorative stonework of the corbelling contrasting with the plain, harled surface of the tower itself. The roughcast, made from Aberdeen granite chips, is of the most luminous pink colour, so that in its rather acid-green setting, Craigievar looks exactly like a fairy-tale castle. The groined vault of the hall is a magnificent specimen of robust 17th-century plaster-work, a geometrical arrangement of broad, richly ornamented bands, the spaces between them being occupied by armorial and emblematic devices while the intersections of the groins are marked by elaborate pendants modelled by hand. Over the fireplace is a huge plaster coat of arms with the inscription 'Doe not valken sleiping dogs'. The tartan carpet was made in Paisley.

86 BALMORAL CASTLE AND THE DEE VALLEY, ABERDEENSHIRE
The royal residence, the largest, but by no means the most fantastic example of the Scottish baronial style, built of Crathie granite and startlingly pale against the sombre fir trees of the surrounding landscape, was begun by William Smith of Aberdeen in 1853, though Prince Albert was responsible for much of the design, details of which are repeated in numerous turreted and castellated granite mansions and hotels along the valley. It was the Prince Consort who had purchased the estate in 1852 from the trustees of the Earl of Fife, and it was he who had planted the conifers which invest

the whole of this part of the Dee valley with such profound melancholy. The land-scape abounds in relics of the first owners of Balmoral. The hills are dotted with cairns commemorating the Royal Family, the most prominent being that to Prince Albert. John Brown's monument, erected to his memory by Queen Victoria, rises con-spicuously in the graveyard of Crathie church, and his house still stands on the other side of the river.

87 GLAMIS CASTLE, ANGUS

The castle dates chiefly from the late 17th century, although the impressive tower incorporates the fabric of a much older building, the fortress popularly supposed to be that of which Duncan is made to say with such terrible irony on the eve of his murder:

> 'This Castle hath a pleasant seat: the air
> Nimbly and sweetly recommends itself
> Unto our gentle senses.'

The bed in which Macbeth was said to have done Duncan to death was among the curiosities shown to visitors in the early 19th century. There is no historical foundation, however, for the setting of the first two acts of *Macbeth* at Glamis. The historical Macbeth did indeed murder Duncan I in 1040, but not at Glamis. Yet he was Thane of Glamis and the castle is associated with events as fearful as those of the play and sufficiently like them to warrant Shakespeare's choice of scene. Malcolm II is said to have been murdered in the vicinity in 1034. And the character of Lady Macbeth may well have been suggested by the crimes attributed, though falsely, to a Lady Glamis of only a generation earlier than the poet's. She was accused of witchcraft and of plotting to poison James V, and was burned at the stake in 1537.

The castle was forfeited to the Crown at her death, but when her innocence was proved, it was restored to her son. It was his descendant, Patrick Lyon, First Earl of Strathmore, who was responsible for the additions and alterations to the castle to which it owes its present form. It belongs to a period when strength and impregnability had long ceased to be the main objectives of the tower-house builder. Traditional severity is here united with a proliferation of battlements, of French-derived corbelling, angle turrets and conical roofs, and with sparse, naively interpreted classical details, lanterns and elongated *œils de bœuf* in the vigorous expression of a purely Scottish fantasy.

88 THE BRUCE TOMB IN THE ABBEY CHURCH, CULROSS, FIFESHIRE

The tomb is that of Sir George Bruce of Carnock who died in 1625. He was famous as the builder of the palace at Culross and for having sunk a coalpit from a bastion in the sea. The tomb is of alabaster and the kneeling figures are portraits of Sir George's

182

sons and daughters. This type of tomb originated in the medieval alabaster workshops some two hundred years before the death of Sir George Bruce, when it became fashionable to place rows of 'weepers' in panels or niches along the sides of the tomb chest on which the effigy of the deceased reclined. These weepers might be either relatives or saints and angels; they were usually shown in the standing position, carved in bold relief, and were, like those on the well-known tomb of Thomas Beauchamp, Earl of Warwick, often remarkable for their liveliness and for the realism with which their dress was represented. In north Britain, even in the Middle Ages, the niches and panels were occasionally omitted and there is an instance at Swine, Yorkshire, of angels carved upon plain, flat slabs and kneeling in pairs on little footstools. The kneeling position became increasingly popular during the 16th century; but while the actual effigy was treated with ever greater naturalism, the weepers were often less differentiated than they had been on earlier tombs, their clothes and features were identical and indicated in the most summary manner, and size alone distinguished the sons and daughters of the departed. The Bruce weepers combine the medieval tradition of individuality and realism with the later conventions to create an effect which can only be compared to some of the strange, hallucinatory repetitions and distortions of an absolutely realistic image found in the most characteristic products of cinematography. The figures are fully three-dimensional, and each is a convincing portrait, yet the female weepers are dressed exactly alike, the intricate details of lace and embroidery rendered and repeated with uncanny accuracy, while two of the male figures wear identical armour and the third appears in civilian dress. But what makes this row of kneeling men and women startlingly surreal is not the uniformity of their dress but the fact that they differ abnormally in size, the three bearded brothers assuming the stature of dwarfs to show they were younger than their sisters.

89 CRATHES CASTLE, KINCARDINESHIRE. PAINTED CEILING

Crathes is famous for the painted ceilings which adorn three of the rooms, the Chamber of the Nine Nobles, the Green Lady's Room and the Chamber of the Nine Muses. The ceiling shown here is that of the last-mentioned of these rooms. In addition to the Muses there are figures of five of the Virtues, Wisdom, Justice, Faith, Hope, and Charity, all clothed in fashionable costume of the time when the work was done, 1599. The scrolls and thistle motifs on the joists were stencilled. Plaster ceilings, such as the one at Craigievar (pl. 85), were rare in 16th- and 17th-century Scotland, but it was not unusual for the open joists and the undersides of floor boards to be embellished with painted designs, even if they were seldom as elaborate as this Crathes ceiling. The sides of the joists and the boards of a room in Gladstone's Land, Lawnmarket, Edinburgh, are decorated with painted panels containing floral patterns and with a repeating design on the undersides of the joists of the same type as that in the Chamber of the Nine Muses.

90 THE CHAPEL ROYAL, FALKLAND PALACE, FIFESHIRE

Romantic Falkland near the shores of Loch Lomond was a hunting palace of the Stuarts. It was begun by James II in the mid-15th century on the site of an earlier castle, but the present aspect of the exterior, of high architectural interest even though so much of it is ruinous, is due mainly to James V. He died of melancholy at Falkland in 1542, aged only thirty, a week after he had received news of the birth of the daughter who was to become Mary, Queen of Scots. The last Stuart king to use Falkland as his hunting home was James VI. Charles I paid a brief visit to the palace when he came to Scotland to be crowned in 1633, and Charles II stayed twice at Falkland, in 1650 and 1651 during the Civil War. After his defeat by the Roundheads he never returned to Scotland, the Stuart kings saw Falkland no more, and the palace itself, despoiled by Cromwell's troops, who occupied it and felled the oaks of the Forest of Falkland where the Stuarts had hunted, fell into decay.

> Fare weill Faulkland, the fortress of Fyfe
> Thy polite park under the Lowmound law,
> Sum tyme in thee I led ane lustie lyfe
> The fallow deir to see them raike in row.

The words of the poet, Sir David Lindsay of the Mount, friend of James V, written after the death of the King, conjure up the atmosphere of Falkland as potently as the mysterious rhyme associated with Hardwick and written at almost exactly the same time, expresses the spirit of that magical house:

> The redolent smelle of eglantine
> We stagges exalt to the Divine.

At Falkland, as at Hardwick, Renaissance motifs are combined with traditional elements in a wholly individual, lively composition. One façade of the Chapel Royal, which is part of the restored South Range of the palace, faces the High Street of the little town of Falkland with castellations and buttresses united to square-headed windows and a distinctly horizontal design. Each buttress bears the figure of an angel in the Late Gothic style supporting a shield bearing an emblem of the Passion, but each buttress is also adorned with canopied niches containing the battered remains of draped statues which are clearly Renaissance work. Two of them are sufficiently well preserved to show the surprising sophistication of the carving. They date from about 1539 and the artist was a Fleming. In the façade looking onto the inner court of the

184

palace, Renaissance elements preponderate. The fabric is of smoothly dressed stone, and though the building is buttressed, as on the outer side, the buttresses are accompanied by classical columns, and between the upper windows the wall is decorated with busts in roundels in the French Renaissance style representing classical mythological figures. The French influence at Falkland is not unexpected, for James's Queen was Mary of Lorraine, and several French craftsmen are recorded as having worked on the palace. They were Jean Marilyone and Nicholas Roy, both master masons, and Hector Beato, a plasterer; one Scottish wright, John Drummond, had been trained in France. It was Nicholas Roy who carved the medallion busts in the courtyard. The architect in charge of the building operations (though the word 'architect' was not used before 1536) was first Sir James Hamilton of Finnart, a natural son of the Earl of Arran, and then John Scrymgeour, the king's Sergeant-at-Arms.

In the interior of the palace it is only in the chapel that the work done in the 16th century survives, though here there is much restoration, carried out at the end of the last century by the Marquess of Bute when he reconstituted the South Range. The photograph shows, in the foreground, the 16th-century hand-turned oak entrance screen, for which John Drummond was probably responsible; on the left, inside the chapel, can be seen the royal pew, pieced together by Lord Bute from decayed fragments. The wall paintings, which are original, include illusionist latticed windows. This decoration dates from the visit to Falkland of Charles I in 1633, but it replaced paintings of the same themes executed in 1537–40. The ribbed ceiling, restored as recently as 1952, was also repainted in 1633, to a pattern originating in the reign of James V. It is a strapwork design displaying Stuart and Tudor royal badges, to which the initials of King Charles, Queen Henrietta Maria, and Charles, Prince of Wales were added during the repainting in 1633.

91 ST MARY'S CHURCH, GRANDTULLY, PERTHSHIRE. THE CEILING
The contrast between the crowded, exuberant painting on the boards of this ceiling and the isolated position of the church in a spacious undulating landscape of vast, almost hedgeless fields and few trees is stimulating and unforgettable. The painting is rather later in date than those at Crathes Castle and presents an intriguing display of Renaissance and medieval motifs combined with Scottish strapwork. In the centre in a painted pedimented frame flanked by vine-encircled pilasters is a picture of primitive intensity. It shows a Resurrection, with nudes starting from their graves, taking place beside a death-bed scene in which Death, a skeleton with a huge arrow in his hand, is approaching a man wearing a fur-trimmed night-cap, lying in a massive four-poster; the diapered floor of the room is rendered with delightful disregard of perspective. High overhead angels seated on clouds sound the Last Trump on either side of a

gigantic sun. From this picture painted ribs run at right angles to form compartments with medallions at the intersections containing the arms of the 'Earle of Atholl', 'Dame Agneis Moncrieff', the 'Earle of Grantully', the 'Duke of Lennox', and pictures of the Evangelists and other saints. Nude angels and naturalistic birds perch on the scrolls and strapwork coiling about the medallions, and the compartments between the ribs are filled with fruits and flowers, emblems of abundance, fulfilment, and peace.

92 KING'S COLLEGE CHAPEL, ABERDEEN

The chapel is all that survives of the original college buildings which were set round a quadrangle. The proportions of the immensely broad low tower in relation to the rest of the building would be visually remarkable if the group boasted no other distinguishing feature, but the design of the upper stage of the tower is so arresting that the eye is at first aware of nothing else. A lantern surmounts arches springing from the four corners of the tower to form a huge crown of stone, encrusted with carved ornament. The tower, dating with the rest of the chapel from 1500–95, was originally topped by a short Gothic spire which collapsed in a great gale on 7th February, 1663. The crown, the work of a local mason, George Thomson, closely resembles that of St Giles's Cathedral in Edinburgh and that too was probably the creation of George Thomson. This strange, exciting form is peculiar to Scotland. Another extraordinary detail of this building is the round-headed west window filled with Flamboyant tracery, dwarfing the small round-headed west door from which it is divided only by a string course.

The interior of the chapel is enriched by magnificent carved oak stalls of Flemish workmanship and here are the tombs of the founder and first Chancellor of King's College, Bishop William Elphinstone who died in 1514, and of its first Principal, Hector Boece. The college was dedicated by its founder to St Mary of the Nativity, but takes its present name from James IV.

93 ST JOHN STREET, PERTH

Perth is a royal burgh, founded by William the Lion in 1210, and was the capital of Scotland until about 1452. Its plan is interesting in that it is a grid pattern of great regularity resembling that of many French towns laid out in the 13th century. Although it cannot rival Edinburgh New Town, Perth boasts a number of severe classical terraces in the neighbourhood of St John Street, well suited to its original rigid layout, built in the late 18th and early 19th centuries. It was in one of these terraces that Ruskin spent part of his childhood and he gives an enchanting description of the town, the banks of the Tay with its swirls of smooth blackness unflecked by foam, and of the Rose Terrace house, in *Praeterita*. Before living in Rose Terrace he had spent each summer with an aunt who had a house at Bridge-end and a garden full of gooseberry bushes sloping steeply down to the river, 'which eddied, three or four feet deep, of sombre crystal, round the steps where the servants dipped their pails'.

The building in the foreground of the photograph is St John's Church. It was founded in 1126 but the present cruciform structure, very much restored, dates chiefly from the 15th century. Here in 1559 John Knox preached the famous sermon on 'purging the churches from idolatry' which was the beginning of the disastrous icono-clastic outburst in Scotland. Prince Charles Stewart attended service at St John's in September 1745 when he spent a week in Perth on his victorious march via Stirling to Edinburgh.

94 THE VICTORIA GATE, DUNDEE, ANGUS

Built in 1844 for a royal visit, this fantastic arch is one of the most assured and memorable works of the Gothic Revival. This is no slavish imitation but a free and vigorous interpretation of medieval motifs drawn from the Norman, Early English, and Perpendicular periods, combined with a composition based on that of the Roman triumphal arch. The base of the structure in fact resembles that of the Arch of Con-stantine in Rome. But instead of completing his arch with a classical entablature, the designer has created an exotic outline by surmounting the principal opening with twin towers which rival the most exuberant inventions of the early Gothic Revivalists in their totally unexpected juxtaposition of forms. Both towerlets consist of a Perpen-dicular octagonal font bowl raised by means of broaches upon eight columns joined by intersecting arcading. The builder's delightfully uninhibited attitude of mind is again shown in his bold use of a double row of gigantic zigzags in the first and third tiers of arcading.

95 THE DOCKS, ABERDEEN

Viewed in a burst of sunshine after rain as the light catches the scales of mica in the granite embankment, the busy port assumes a poetical aspect not often associated with this harsh city of stone on its cold estuarine site. The harbour is at once the centre of Aberdeen's industrial development, playing a vital part in Britain's economy, and a place of fascinating historical associations. When Eysteinn the Viking 'brought his ships to the town of Apardion' in the 12th century, he sailed through what is now the Tidal Harbour, Victoria Dock and Upper Dock and launched his attack on the burgh which had grown up on the tidal mud-flat known as the Green, formed by a loop of the Denburn at its mouth. It was along the north bank of the Denburn that the first wharf was built some time during the 13th century. It was called the 'peere' and was extended eastwards during the Middle Ages and again in 1623. On this stretch James Street, Sugarhouse Lane, Mearns Street, and part of Commerce Street were laid out, and the present Virginia Street follows the line of the former 'Fittie-gait', a grassy lane of such smoothness that it became known as the 'carpet-walk'. On summer evenings young Aberdonians would 'walk-the-carpet', a phrase which was eventually used to describe similar strolls along Union Street. The development of the harbour was hampered by two natural obstacles, the 'gryt barre', a fluctuating sand barrier, and the 'knock metellan', a large rock embedded in the centre of the navigable channel. Prayers and fasting had long been tried in vain as remedies when, in 1607, it was decided to build a bulwark at the mouth of the Dee, where the so-called Torry harbour was sited. This 'peere of Torrie' was a dry-stone structure reinforced by massive oak beams, and much of the work was carried out by the citizens themselves, encouraged in their labours, like modern factory hands, by music, for 'Andro Inglis, the swesch-man (or drummer) and Jasper Mylne, the common piper' were paid £5 Scots and 10 merks respectively for 'thair extraordinary paines dureing the bigging of the bull-warke'. In 1610 the 'knock metellan' was removed by David Anderson of Finzeauch, a mathematician, by the incredibly simple expedient of securing a number of empty casks to the rock at low tide and towing it away when the water rose.

In the subsequent development of the port the famous engineers Smeaton, Rennie, and Telford all played a part. The main events in the harbour's history were the laying-out of Marischal Street in 1768 to give direct access to the port from the city centre, the diversion of the estuary of the Dee, the reclaiming of the islands or 'inches' dividing the estuaries of the Denburn and the Dee and the building of Victoria Bridge.

The chief industries associated with the Aberdeen docks are of course fishing and shipbuilding. A brisk trade in the export of cured salmon, trout, and other fish was already going on between Aberdeen and the Continent in the Middle Ages. The herring industry is still one of the most lucrative sources of revenue in the burgh. The ancient industry of shipbuilding reached its spectacular peak in the 19th century with the introduction of iron and steam. It was then that the famous Aberdeen clippers, the *Cairngorm*, the *Chrysolite*, and the *Thermopylae*, engaged in those thrilling China tea races with their American rivals which are recorded in Currier and Ives's prints and pictured on Staffordshire plates of the period.

96 DAVIOT, INVERNESS-SHIRE

The trim, whitewashed church is a most unexpected sight in the wild, stony land-scape of Strath Nairn. It is dated 1826 and delightfully fuses Gothic tradition with the neo-classical style. The tower, placed in an unorthodox position at the east end of the church, combines extreme verticality with classical balls, obelisks, *œils de bœuf*, and round-headed windows, while the simple, aisleless nave, lit by Palladian windows, is battlemented and buttressed, although the buttresses have been camouflaged by classical mouldings.

97 OLD LEANACH COTTAGE, CULLODEN, INVERNESS-SHIRE

This traditional cottage, roofed by primitive thatch held in place by stones attached to the ends of ropes, stands in isolation on Culloden Moor, the setting in 1746 of the last major battle in Britain, when the last Jacobite rising under Prince Charles was quelled by the Duke of Cumberland. The cottage survived the battle and was continuously inhabited until 1912 when its owner, a Miss Bell MacDonald, died there, aged 83. Her grandmother, who had lived in another cottage near by, had been a child at the time of the battle. There was then a barn attached to the cottage, which was the scene of one of the most savage of the many atrocities which followed on the defeat of the Jacobites. Some thirty Highlanders, several of them wounded, had taken refuge in the barn and were discovered there by Cumberland's men two days later. The soldiers were ordered to barricade the barn and set fire to it. All thirty of Charles's supporters perished horribly in the flames.

The battle took place on 16th April. Prince Charles would have been captured shortly afterwards but for Flora MacDonald, who disguised him as her maid and brought him safely to Skye. Eventually on 21st September, after several narrow escapes, he sailed for France accompanied by many of his followers.

The results of the battle were more tragic for Scotland than the struggle itself. It might even be said that the Highlands have never entirely recovered from those events of more than two hundred years ago. Soon after the Jacobite defeat Acts of Parliament were passed to prohibit the wearing of Highland Dress or the use of tartan; the playing of bagpipes was forbidden; the Episcopal Church was severely restricted and Catholics were debarred from holding any public office. In 1747 another law was designed to destroy the political and social system of Scotland. This was the Act for the Abolition of Heritable Jurisdictions, which formed the basis of Scottish local government. Thirty years afterwards when he was touring the Highlands, Dr Johnson summed up the results of these Acts in a quotation from Tacitus: 'They have created a desert and have called it peace.' The chiefs had fled abroad; sheep, belonging to English landlords, were grazing among the ruins of ancestral homes; the stream of emigrants, which was to reach huge proportions after the Napoleonic Wars, had begun to flow towards Canada, whence in 1829 an exiled Highlander wrote the following song:

> From the lone shieling of the misty island
> Mountains divide us and the waste of seas—
> Yet still the blood is strong, the heart is Highland,
> And we in dreams behold the Hebrides.

When the bold kindred, in time long vanish'd
Conquered the soil and fortified the keep—
No seer foretold the children would be banish'd,
That a degenerate lord might boast his sheep.

98 STONES OF CLAVA, INVERNESS-SHIRE

These strange monuments, the most complete of their kind in Britain, are to be seen about a mile from the famous battlefield of Culloden, on the far side of the river Nairn. They consist of three cairns, each surrounded by a circle of standing stones. Two of the cairns, including the one shown here, contain chambers approached by an entrance passage, while the third conceals a chamber with no entrance. They date from between 3000 and 2000 B.C.

99 CASTLE URQUHART, LOCH NESS, INVERNESS-SHIRE

Loch Ness is one of the magnificent lakes that form a chain along the valley of the Great Glen which runs from north-east to south-west across Scotland, cutting off the Northern Highlands from the rest of the country. The lake is of astonishing and nearly uniform depth: its common soundings are 750 to 800 feet and its extreme depth is 900 feet. Like all the other lakes in the Great Glen, it is fringed by a narrow shelf of rock, beyond which it suddenly deepens. Because of its curious formation and unusual depth the cold surface water is continually replaced, as its increased specific gravity causes it to sink, by warmer strata of water; and so Loch Ness has never been known to freeze. In severe weather steam can be seen to rise from the lake, and earlier genera-tions of travellers, taking steam for smoke, assumed the existence of a hidden fire in the bowels of the earth beneath the water. This belief seemed to be dramatically confirmed when on the day of the great earthquake at Lisbon, 1st November, 1755, the waters of Loch Ness rose and, rushing violently to the south-west, continued to ebb and flow for more than an hour. At the precise time of a second earthquake on 13th August, 1816, the men on board a dredging barge moored at the south-western end of Loch Ness were alarmed by a rumbling sound which appeared to come from the heart of the lake, although they were not sensible of any unnatural motion in the water.

From its steep promontory Castle Urquhart commands a view of the whole lake. The water washes the eastern wall of the fortress, and the photograph shows the strong ramparts, ditch, and drawbridge with which it was once defended. When entire the castle could accommodate 600 men. In the early Middle Ages it was one of the principal seats of the once powerful Comyns. In 1303 it fell to Edward I, who reinforced it. In 1509 it was granted by James IV, along with the estate and baronry of Urquhart to the Lairds of Grant, who held the castle for four centuries.

100 KILMONIVAIG CHURCH, GLEN SPEAN, INVERNESS-SHIRE

The wooded valley of the Spean where the river spreads out over a rocky channel, abounding in tiny cataracts and swirling about little tree-covered islands, and the isolated Victorian church of Kilmonivaig with its cluster of granite tombstones, are grandly confronted by the northern precipices of Ben Nevis (4,406 ft), the highest mountain in the British Isles, whitened by snow even in July, when this photograph was taken. The view well illustrates the Rev. William Gilpin's conception of the part a mountain could play in a Picturesque composition:

A mountain is of use sometimes to close a distance by an elegant, varied line; and sometimes to come in a second ground, hanging over a lake, or forming a skreen to the nearest objects. To each purpose the Scotch mountains are well adapted. The distances of this country, with all their uniformity, have at least one praise, as we have often had occasion to observe, that of being bounded by a grand chain of blue mountains: and when these mountains approach, their shapes are generally such as may with little alteration be transferred to canvas.

Observations on Several Parts of Great Britain,
particularly the Highlands of Scotland. 1789.

The top of Ben Nevis is the wettest place in Scotland, with a rainfall, or snowfall, of 151 inches a year.

101 HIGHLAND BULL IN THE PARK OF BALAVIL, NEAR KINGUSSIE, INVERNESS-SHIRE

He might have posed for Landseer. He is recognisable chiefly by the width of his horns and his small size. Cattle were the great wealth of the Highlands and were formerly always, like this bull, very dark, almost black in colour, not the shaggy light brown of what are popularly called 'Highland cattle' to-day.

The mansion of Balavil was built by James Macpherson (*see* note 81), alleged translator of Ossian's poems. It was later inhabited by the scientist Sir David Brewster, who married Macpherson's daughter.

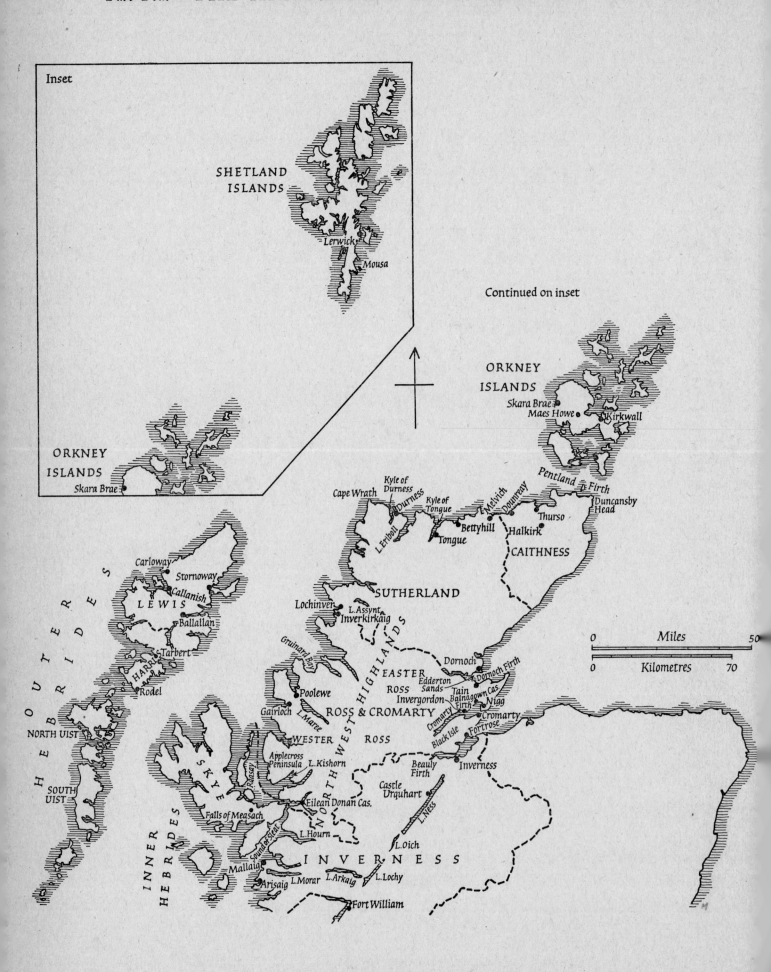

Part Four THE HIGHLANDS AND ISLANDS

Inset

SHETLAND ISLANDS

Lerwick

Mousa

Continued on inset

ORKNEY ISLANDS

Skara Brae
Maes Howe
Kirkwall

ORKNEY ISLANDS

Skara Brae

Cape Wrath

Kyle of Durness
Durness

Kyle of Tongue

Melvich
Dounreay

Pentland Firth

Duncansby Head

Thurso

L.Eriboll

Tongue
Bettyhill

Halkirk

CAITHNESS

Carloway

Stornoway

Callanish

LEWIS

Ballallan

Tarbert

HARRIS

Rodel

OUTER HEBRIDES

NORTH UIST

SOUTH UIST

SUTHERLAND

Lochinver
L.Assynt
Inverkirkaig

Gruinard Bay

Poolewe

Gairloch

L.Maree

WESTER ROSS

Applecross Peninsula
L.Kishorn

SKYE

Raasay

Falls of Measach

Eilean Donan Cas.

Sound of Sleat

L.Hourn

Mallaig

Arisaig
L.Morar
L.Arkaig
L.Lochy

INVERNESS

Fort William

NORTH WEST HIGHLANDS

EASTER ROSS

ROSS & CROMARTY

Edderton Sands

Dornoch
Dornoch Firth

Tain
Balnagown Cas.
Nigg

Invergordon

Cromarty Firth
Cromarty

Black Isle
Fortrose

Beauly Firth
Inverness

Castle Urquhart

L.Ness

L.Oich

INNER HEBRIDES

Miles
0   50

Kilometres
0   70

103

104

107

108

109

110

111

113

114

116

117

121

122

102 CROMARTY FIRTH FROM NIGG, EASTER ROSS

On the far side of the water, Ben Wyvis rises abruptly from the lowland woods and the same rich farmland as that which fills the foreground of the photograph with waving corn. The contrast between wild, mountainous scenery, territory inhabited only by the sheep farmer, and stretches of tillable land is characteristic of Ross. The land to the east of this county is some of the best-farmed arable land in Scotland.

103 ST MARTIN'S CROSS, IONA, HEBRIDES

Iona belongs to one of the two southernmost groups of the Hebrides and lies off the coast of Argyll, just north of the Firth of Lorne. The island was a centre of Druid worship long before St Columba landed here after he had, for reasons which remain uncertain, left his native Ireland in 593. The Saint's biographer, Adamnan, called the island Ioua, which was later changed by a monkish scribe to the more euphonious Iona; but for centuries it was known also as Icolmkill—the Island of the Cell of Columba—a name which expresses those intimate connections with the Early Christian Saint which seem part of the extraordinarily clear light and colour of this Hebridean island. It was, according to Dr Johnson, 'the luminary of the Caledonian regions, whence savage clans and roving barbarians derived the benefits of knowledge and the blessings of religion', and, again in the words of Dr Johnson, Iona is a place where 'to abstract the mind from all local emotion would be impossible if it were endeavoured and would be foolish if it were possible'.

St Columba landed with twelve companions and established an eremitical monastery of the informal type found in Ireland. Recent excavations have revealed the general position and extent of the original enclosure, though many of the early buildings lie beneath the medieval remains and are thus not accessible to the spade. Traces of a small square hut have been discovered on the rocky outcrop of Tor Abb, immediately to the west of the church, and it is conjectured that this may have been the cell of St Columba himself. His community rapidly became one of the most celebrated in western Christendom and was responsible for the conversion of the Northern Picts and the inhabitants of the Orkneys, Shetlands, and Iceland. St Columba died on Iona, before the altar, it is said, after thirty years of unceasing activity.

The granite cross of St Martin belongs to a much later period than that of the Saint. It closely resembles the preaching crosses of Ireland, and like them was probably inspired by the work of the Northumbrian carvers, such as the Ruthwell Cross (pl. 40). It must be two hundred years later at least than the Ruthwell Cross and probably dates, like the crosses at Clonmacnois and Monasterboice, from the 10th century. At that time the monastery and its church had been destroyed by the Vikings who raided Iona again and again during the 9th century. Pilgrims would gather round the cross, near the ruins of St Columba's church, the preacher taking his text from the scenes sculp-tured upon it. St Martin's Cross conforms to the same basic pattern as the Irish crosses. It is set on a rectangular base in the shape of a truncated pyramid, and takes the form of a four-sided shaft with a cross-bar, and a wheel (a cosmic symbol) surrounding the intersection. This and the splendid Kildalton Cross are the only two crosses with wheel heads still standing in Scotland. The carvings on the principal face of the shaft very closely resemble those on the crosses at Monasterboice and Clonmacnois, though they are more roughly executed. They consist of a series of reliefs of scenes of the Passion —not, however, separated here, as in the Irish examples, by mouldings. The face seen in the photograph is adorned merely with decorative reliefs of Celtic character.

104 THE CATHEDRAL, IONA, HEBRIDES. NORTH DOOR OF THE CHANCEL
The present cathedral dates from the early 13th century when Reginald, son of Somerlyd, Lord of the Isles, founded a new Benedictine abbey on the site of St Columba's monastery, adding an Augustinian nunnery a few years later. The Benedic-tine church served as the cathedral of the see of Sodor under the primacy of Trondheim in Norway until the second half of the 15th century, when, in 1499, it became the cathedral church of the Scottish diocese of the Isles. Much of the fabric was restored or rebuilt at that time. At the Dissolution in 1578 the cathedral was dismantled and, according to local tradition, some three hundred stone crosses were flung into the sea.

In 1899 the eighth Duke of Argyll presented the cathedral ruins to the Church of Scotland on the unique condition that any recognised Christian denomination might apply for its use for the celebration of its full office of worship. The building was

210

restored between 1902 and 1910, and the Iona Community, which was established in 1938 by Dr George Macleod of the notorious Govan district in Glasgow and consists chiefly of craftsmen and newly ordained ministers, has since undertaken the restoration of the monastic buildings adjoining the cathedral.

The doorway shown in the photograph is a most interesting and characteristic example of the stylistic peculiarities of Scottish architecture in remote parts of the country at the time of the extensive building operations of the 15th century. No attempt has been made to introduce the conventional late Gothic forms; and if it were not for the trefoil-headed arch it would be almost impossible to date this opening. The new work is closely modelled on the old, the capitals are still Romanesque in shape and the carved decoration, typical of that of the West Highland School, includes revived Romanesque and Transitional motifs.

105 CASTLE STALKER, APPIN, ARGYLLSHIRE

The tower-house on its offshore rock at the mouth of Loch Laich was built by the Stewarts of Appin in the late 15th century to receive James IV. The intensity of the light and colour of this scene on a fine day is so overwhelming that it could scarcely be borne without the frequent interruption of cloud and rain. The tonal values seem to be accentuated as if seen in the convex Claude glass once carried by landscape painters.

This district is associated with the Appin Murder upon which R. L. Stevenson based part of the plot of *Kidnapped*. The unpopular Campbell of Glenure was shot from behind a dyke in 1752 and the local laird, James Stewart of the Glens, was arrested and hanged at Ballachulish Ferry after an unfair trial by a Campbell judge and a Campbell jury. The real culprit would have given himself up, but was persuaded by the populace that it would be a vain sacrifice as the Campbells were bent on the destruction of James Stewart.

106 THE FALLS OF MEASACH, WESTER ROSS

The cascade is seen from the near-by suspension bridge. It is the narrowness and depth of the gorge through which the water is forced which makes these Falls remarkable, especially after rain when the awe-inspiring fury of the yellow-foaming torrent hurtling through the tree-shaded canyon recalls Gray's words after visiting the Highlands:

'I do not remember to have gone ten paces without an exclamation that there was no restraining. There are certain scenes that would awe an atheist into belief. . . . One need not have a fantastic imagination to see spirits here at noonday.'

Behind the cataract can be seen the craggy slopes of the immense mountain range of An Teallach, of which again Gray wrote in a letter to Mason:

'The mountains are ecstatic and ought to be visited in pilgrimage once a year. None but those monstrous creatures of God know how to join so much beauty with so much horror. A fig for your poets, painters, gardeners and clergymen that have not been among them; their imaginations can be made up of nothing but bowling-greens, flowering shrubs, horse ponds, Fleet ditches, shell grottoes and Chinese rails. What a pity it is I cannot draw nor describe.'

107 STAFFA, HEBRIDES

Though its circumference scarcely exceeds 1½ miles, uninhabited Staffa is, on account of its extraordinary geological formation, one of the best known of the Hebridean islands. It only became familiar to the outer world, however, after it was visited in 1772 by Sir Joseph Banks who had heard of its unique basaltic formation from an Irishman, a Mr Leach. He concentrated his attention particularly on Fingal's Cave, making careful notes of all its dimensions, which were afterwards published in Pennant's *Tour in Scotland*, 1775. The name of the island is Norse and means Stave Island, for the strange hexagonal columns of black basalt of which Staffa is composed are reminiscent of the vertically set tree-logs of which the Norsemen built their stave houses. The formation is due to repeated and violent volcanic action in Tertiary times, when pressure upon cooling basalt caused it to assume these prismatic shapes. The gigantic eruption followed a line through Staffa, Mull, Islay and Rathlin across to the Giant's Causeway in Co. Antrim. The photograph shows part of a similar causeway and the islet of Buchaille, visible only at low tide, where the basalt columns are curiously curved and distorted. Near by is the celebrated Fingal's Cave, called in Gaelic *Uaimh Binn*, the musical cave. It is the most astonishing of the caves which riddle the perpendicular south and west façades of Staffa. It is not surprising that it should have appealed especially to the Picturesque traveller, for the entrance resembles a Gothic arch and in the amazing interior nature seems to have been ordered by art, so regular are the stupendous columns that line the walls, so symmetrical, yet subtly varied, the groupings. But of all the distinguished visitors to Staffa, none has caught the wild atmosphere of its Atlantic setting and the rhythm of its Cyclopean architecture more vividly than Mendelssohn in his 'Hebrides' overture. Though ruined by over-familiarity, it remains one of the finest pieces of descriptive music ever written, and anyone who has entered the Cave and walked on Staffa will at once realise that it exactly corresponds to the mood of the place as it is revealed also in this photograph.

108 GRUINARD BAY, WESTER ROSS

This lonely bay, facing north, is wonderfully expressive of the geology and miraculous light of Wester Ross. Gleaming quartzite mingles with red sandstone and hard unyielding gneiss, and beyond the ochre and brown, the acid green scrub and grey-green water of the foreground, the hills look for a moment bone-white against charcoal black, changing almost instantly to gleaming silver and grape-purple behind a sea of gunmetal.

109 TARBERT, HARRIS, HEBRIDES

The shattered hulk of the ship in the foreground of the photograph might be the emblem of the Atlantic Hebrides, ravaged by sea and wind. Much of the island is a rocky waste, and it is a testimony to the resolution of the people that Harris is so well inhabited to-day. Harris is very nearly two islands, and Tarbert (a Norse word meaning a neck of land where boats can be dragged across from sea to sea) stands on the narrow waist, only half a mile wide, between North and South Harris. The cottages face south and most of them have tiny gardens bursting with flowers in defiance of the naked hills stretching along the coast. The majority of the people are crofters and lobster fishers, with weaving and knitting as subsidiary industries.

110 BALALLAN, LEWIS, HEBRIDES

The photograph shows one of the strangest features of the Outer Hebrides, the black moor of Lewis. It is a dark brown peat bog laced with hundreds of tiny lochs, sometimes clear and colourless as mirrors, sometimes blacker than the surrounding peat, fathomless and mysterious, and then again, a piercing blue, ruffled by the wind. The moor is not flat but full of slopes and hollows where one or two cows can be grazed in summer. During the last decade, Lewis men have reclaimed about 10,000 acres of moorland and along the west coast patches of green as well as blue stand out against the black moor. Between sea and moorland lie little townships like Balallan, where the houses sit widely spaced on their green crofts. The system of holding is a hereditary one, where a strip of arable land is combined with rights of common grazing on the moor. The crofter's right to occupy and cultivate his croft descends from father to son or can be willed away. For although the crofter holds his land on a yearly tenancy, the landlord cannot give him notice to quit if he pays his rent and cultivates his land. A croft is seldom more than five acres in extent and is never the crofter's sole support. He must always find additional work such as fishing or weaving. It is especially typical of Lewis that new and old houses stand side by side, a stark white, one- or sometimes two-storeyed rectangle of cemented walls roofed with corrugated iron or slate, keeping company with an abandoned thatched and windowless 'black house', often used, as here, as a byre.

111 TORRIN, SKYE, HEBRIDES

The Vikings gave the island its name, Skuyö, meaning Isle of Cloud. Behind the crofter's modern cottage rises the conical shape of one of the volcanic mountains, the Cuillin, for which Skye is famous. The name is not connected with the legendary Irish hero Cuchullin, but derives from the old Norse kjöllen, meaning 'keel-shaped ridges'. The range is of naked rock, astonishingly harsh and dark (the Black Cuillin) or dusky red, changing for fleeting, incredible moments in a June sunset to flaming crimson (the Red Cuillin). The material is coarse, crystalline gabbro, exposed by erosion.

112 CALLANISH, LEWIS, HEBRIDES. SMALL STONE CIRCLE

After Stonehenge, the megaliths of Callanish are the most important in Britain and in their untamed setting on a peninsula jutting out into East Loch Roag, they are far more impressive than the Salisbury Plain monument, fenced in, labelled and thronged by tourists. The Callanish stones probably date from between 2000 and 1500 BC and constitute the largest Temple of the Sun in Scotland. The circle shown here is one of two standing to the east of the major monument, a huge ring of thirteen monoliths set at a 37-foot diameter round a great central stone some 17 feet high with, leading up to it, an avenue 90 yards long and 9 yards wide marked by stones 6 feet high. Single rows of stone radiate east, west and south of the Circle. The site was excavated in 1857–58 by Sir James Matheson, who discovered a chambered cairn beside the central pillar, perhaps a communal tomb. Herodotus refers to the Callanish stones as 'The Great Winged Temple of the Northern Isles'.

113 ST CLEMENT'S CHURCH, RODIL, HARRIS, HEBRIDES

The church standing on the southernmost point of Harris is built of local gneiss and wonderfully expressive of the desert of outcropping gneiss which forms the east coast of South Harris. Although, except for the square-headed windows of the nave, it looks so primitive and is so entirely medieval in feeling, St Clement's is not mentioned before 1549, a short time after it had perhaps been rebuilt on the site of an earlier foundation. Rodil was the burial place of the MacLeod chiefs of Dunvegan and it may have been built by one of them. The church is a cruciform building with transepts and a tiny choir. On the exterior of the tower are some small ornamental carvings, the subjects of which, Sheelanagigs (fertility symbols), are of pre-Christian and Norse origin, and so shock the islanders that St Clement's is never entered except by strangers.

114 ST CLEMENT'S CHURCH, RODIL, HARRIS, HEBRIDES. THE TOMB OF
ALASDAIR CROTACH

Alasdair Crotach, the seventh MacLeod chief, caused this tomb to be prepared for himself in 1528, twenty years before his death. It is an expression of personal taste

214

uninfluenced in this remote spot by fashionable trends, and the knightly effigy might easily be taken for a medieval carving. It is of black schist and from the style of the subject's armour and the position of his hands, it could be early 15th-century work, although the detail, owing to the intractability of the material, is undeniably coarse. The character of the reliefs adorning the wall and gabled canopy above the figure is equally misleading. The panel of St Michael and Satan weighing souls immediately above the knight and the panels of apostles and angels round the outer edge of the arch are Romanesque in feeling, while the carving of the Trinity on the keystone, in which the subject is treated in the traditional way with God the Father holding the Crucifix between His knees, resembles the treatment of the same subject on a 15th-century tomb at Willoughby-on-the-Wold, Nottinghamshire. The triptych-like arrangement of the Virgin and Child flanked by St Clement and a Bishop on the inner wall also recalls this Nottinghamshire tomb, though the Skye relief is cruder. The carving above this group, of trumpeting angels on either side of a sun and the hunting scene and three stags below the triptych, have much in common with the plasterwork of the deceased's own period.

115 St Magnus's Cathedral, Kirkwall, Orkney. The chancel
    and transept

Earl Magnus, the warrior poet of Orkney, was treacherously murdered by his cousin Haakon in 1115 and his heir and nephew Earl Rognvald built the cathedral in 1137 to commemorate him. The remains of both Magnus and Rognvald were discovered in 1925 in pinewood chests enclosed in two pillars on either side of the original altar. The see was under the archdiocese of Trondheim until 1472 and both culturally and politically Orkney, as its very name testifies, was part of the Norse world. Magnus and Rognvald were themselves Norse earls. Yet the cathedral shows the Anglo-Norman influence of the Durham School, which may have been due to Rognvald's friendship with Bishop William the Old. St Magnus's is a relatively small building, yet such is the nobility of its proportions, such the massive severity of its cylindrical pillars and rhythmic arches, that it makes a more overwhelming impression of grandeur than Dunfermline Abbey, with which it has much in common. The cathedral was not completed for three centuries; the oldest part of the building is seen in the photograph and dates from the mid twelfth century.

116 The Tolbooth or Town House, Tain, Easter Ross

It was in the Tolbooth that the public affairs of the Scottish burgh were transacted. Here the burgh court and council met and here too was the municipal prison. The design of the Tolbooth was originally based on that of the tower house for similar reasons of security; and usually, as here, the building was surmounted by angle turrets and a belfry, where the town bell was housed. Tain Tolbooth is one of the few examples of the tower-house type to survive and even so the fabric is not all original. It was built at about the end of the 16th century and much restored in 1707-27.

117 DORNOCH CATHEDRAL, SUTHERLAND

Though it only boasts a population of 800, Dornoch is the capital of the wild county of Sutherland, was once the seat of the Bishop of Caithness, and is dominated by its high-roofed cathedral. That part of the fabric shown in the foreground of the photograph, the noble piers of the crossing, is, together with the chancel, all that survives in a comparatively unaltered state of the church begun in *c.* 1224 by Gilbert of Moravia. The nave is the work of William Burn (*see also* pl. 19), carried out in 1835-37, when the church was in a state of neglect; it had never recovered from the damage inflicted during the attack on the Bishop's Castle in 1570 by the Master of Caithness and Mackay of Strathnaver. Burn, the author of the successful choir of Dunfermline Abbey Church, revived the Early English character of the building without obtruding any of his own considerable fantasy in the design. The five-light west window with its simple bar tracery, a form common in this part of Scotland, is particularly convincing. Yet there is a mechanical precision about this interior which is alien to the Middle Ages but which at once establishes it as coeval with the marble statue by Chantrey at the end of the aisle commemorating the first Duke of Sutherland, who died in 1833.

118 EDDERTON SANDS, DORNOCH FIRTH, EASTER ROSS

The Firth, an arm of the sea some 15 miles long, runs between Easter Ross and Sutherland. At low tide the interplay of light and shade on the rock-broken water is of a clarity and brilliancy of colour found only in the north. The photograph was taken at about 10 p.m. on a long, light-reflecting June evening with larks and cuckoos still singing. Darkness at this season of the year in the northern Highlands is no more than a midnight twilight. During the interminable winter nights of this region the Northern Lights can sometimes be seen from here, a faint glow along the northern horizon or a far-off sweep of pale searchlights. In stormy weather the thunder of giant waves reverberates on Edderton Sands; they are breaking on a sandbank at the mouth of the Firth, known by its Norse name of the Gizzen.

119 THE LIGHTHOUSE, CROMARTY, WESTER ROSS

There were no lighthouses to warn shipping off the coast of Scotland before the creation of the Board of Commissioners of Northern Lighthouses in 1786. The most impressive of the Commissioners' projects was the construction of the Bell Rock

216

Lighthouse off Arbroath in 1807–11, designed by John Rennie. The low tower of the lighthouse at Cromarty is fused with a one-storeyed keeper's lodge in the picturesque Egyptian style which came into fashion in the south soon after Napoleon's campaign in Egypt but did not find its way to the north of Scotland until much later. The lighthouse was in fact built in 1846. Perhaps the common root of the words Pharos and Pharaoh prompted the architect in his choice of style. In the foreground of the photograph can be seen an altar to Aesculapius, physician to the Argonauts.

120 THE TOLBOOTH OR TOWN HOUSE, CROMARTY, EASTER ROSS
The old town of Cromarty, destroyed by sea erosion, was newly built during the second half of the 18th century when a hempen-cloth factory, established by a beneficent local laird, George Ross, had brought a sudden burst of prosperity to the community. The attractive Town House is a characteristic example of the unsophisticated interpretation of the Georgian style which meets the eye everywhere in the centre of the tiny town. The building is also representative of the later type of Town House which combines the traditional tolbooth bell-tower, projecting from the main front, with a plain rectangular symmetrical block. (*See also* pl. 35 and 116).

121 MAES HOWE, MAINLAND, ORKNEY. THE CENTRAL CHAMBER
The tomb of Maes Howe, a huge green mound 115 feet in diameter and 24 feet high stands above the Lochs of Harray and Stenness on Mainland, the largest of the Orkney islands. There is perhaps no other place in the British Isles so strongly and strangely pervaded with the atmosphere of the remote prehistoric past. Just below Maes Howe rise the Standing Stones of Stenness and the circle of unhewn sandstone monoliths known as the Ring of Brogar; sepulchral tumuli emboss the ground; and on the coast a little distance from the far end of Loch Harray lies the Stone Age village of Skara Brae. Maes Howe ('mestr', greatest; 'haugr', mound) has many affinities with the great stone tomb of New Grange in the valley of the Boyne in Ireland and these two monuments are among the finest prehistoric megalithic chamber tombs in Europe. Both are Passage Graves consisting of a passage leading into a central chamber, the passage at Maes Howe being 36 feet long and the central chamber 15 feet square. At both New Grange and Maes Howe three side compartments open out from the walls of the main chamber to give a cruciform plan. Both are surrounded at a distance of some 50 to 70 feet from their base by a broad ditch, in the case of Maes Howe some 45 feet wide and 6 feet deep. Though both tombs are now covered by soil and turf, it is believed that this was the work of time and nature and that these dry-stone buildings were originally left exposed. Architecturally the structures show certain divergencies; for while New Grange is constructed of large upright stones called orthostats and

roofed with a corbelled vault, Maes Howe combines the use of orthostats in its walls with smaller stones most carefully dressed and beautifully fitted together. The walls rise vertically for about 4½ feet and then converge in overlapping courses. There are four corner piers or buttresses, the tops of which have been precisely cut to fit in with the overlapping corbels of the vault. Originally the central chamber which now survives to a height of 12½ feet rose to a height of 18 to 20 feet. The upper part of the roof was removed when the site was excavated in 1861 by Farrer. This difference in construction between the two monuments may be explained by geology, the fine masonry of Maes Howe being the direct result of the availability of the Orkney flagstones which were easily split into smaller pieces, whereas the Boyne valley rock did not lend itself to this treatment. In addition to this distinction in the fabric of the two tombs, New Grange stands apart from nearly all other megalithic monuments on account of the richness and variety of the ornament that covers so many of its stones. The strange face or oculi motif (a representation of the Earth Mother or Mother Goddess), which links New Grange with the tombs of southern Iberia, is however found, if not at Maes Howe itself, in the Orkneys in the chambered cairn on the Holm of Papa Westray. And at Maes Howe the placing of the side chambers, not, as at New Grange, at ground level, but up in the side of the wall, with large blocking stones standing near by which could completely seal the openings, is exactly paralleled at Alcalà in south Portugal. The similarities between the Irish and Orkney burial mounds and the megalithic tombs of southern Iberia have led some archaeologists, among them Dr Glyn Daniel and the late Professor Sean Ó Ríordáin, to suggest that Maes Howe, like New Grange, was built by trading communities from Spain and Portugal who left their homeland some time in the third millennium BC, travelled from Brittany along the west coast of France and Normandy and spread from Ireland and Wales to Scotland and the Orkneys, establishing in all those places their religious customs and beliefs and their methods of building. It is thought that the great mound of Maes Howe was the collective grave of the chiefs of these traders and that it was built either by the descendants or by contemporaries of the architects of New Grange. The date has been given as about 2500 or 2000 BC, though megaliths were being constructed in Europe from the fourth to the first millennium BC.

When Maes Howe was opened in 1861, it was not the first time that it had been disturbed. Earl Rognvald and Eindrid the Younger are usually named as the first intruders. They entered the tomb in 1150-51 when they were wintering in Orkney with an expeditionary force. In 1153 Earl Harold and his men landed at Stromness and sheltered in Maes Howe 'while a snowstorm drove over them, and there two men of their band lost their wits and that was a great hindrance to their journey'. All this is related by 12th-century inscriptions in runes on various stones in the tomb. Four of these inscriptions state that Crusaders broke into the Howe and removed treasure from it; another declares that 'away to the north great treasure is hidden', and yet another names 'Hakin' as having personally removed treasure from Maes Howe and announces that much still lies hidden, awaiting a lucky finder. The Vikings also engraved three figures on the face of the north-eastern pier of the central chamber—a dragon, a walrus, and a serpent knot.

In the popular imagination Maes Howe is still inhabited by the strong but stupid *haug bui* (dweller in the mound), the legendary guardian of the tomb's treasures and secrets.

122 MOUSA BROCH, SHETLAND. INTERIOR

The *Broch* or Pictish stronghold on the island of Mousa, 45 feet high and 50 feet in diameter at the base, is the most complete monument of its kind to survive (*see also* p. 31). The photograph shows the openings to the galleries running between the two concentric walls of the structure. It was taken from a similar opening on the opposite side of the inner wall, reached by a stair. The character of the masonry, close-set stones fitted together without mortar and bonded at heights of about 5 feet with large slabs, can be clearly seen. It is thought that cattle were kept in the inner court of the *broch*, while a single household was accommodated in the galleries and cells between the walls.

123 SKARA BRAE, MAINLAND, ORKNEY

This remarkable Neolithic settlement may, according to Dr Glyn Daniel, be contemporary with Maes Howe. The dry-stone masonry shows the same control over the material, the same combination of monolithic slabs and cut stones. The village consists of seven houses, which owe their unusual state of preservation to the fact that they were buried in sand and completely hidden until in 1850 a storm uncovered some of the masonry. The village was later excavated by Professor V. G. Childe. The houses are connected by galleries; each has a central hearth and inbuilt furniture—stone beds, stone cupboards or dressers—and space for storage let into the floor. The tools, beads, pots, and remains of animals found in the houses suggest two or three periods of occupation. The site had been inhabited long before these stone dwellings were built, for they were discovered to be standing not upon rock or sand, but on the piled debris, shells, bones, peat, and ash of an earlier settlement. Skara Brae appears to have been abandoned because of encroaching sand, and scattered implements found in one of the houses imply that a storm similar to that which revealed the village, may have caused its last inhabitants to flee from it in panic. The bodies of two men, one a youth, the other a greybeard, found buried in sand on top of the houses, hint at a tragic flight from some natural disaster, a Pompeii in miniature.

124 LOCH ASSYNT, SUTHERLAND

The bare mountains of Sutherland are varied by more stretches of water than in any other county of Scotland. The firs on the island in Loch Assynt, suggesting a sudden, unexpected parallel between this northern scene and a typical Japanese landscape, are unusual in this treeless countryside, except in the glens. But Loch Assynt is noted for its vegetation, especially its alpine flowers and ferns. It is difficult to associate such rich plant life with the northern Highlands—as difficult as it is to fathom the logic which led to the calling of this northern extremity of our island Sutherland. It was given its name by a people from regions yet farther to the north—the Norse settlers in Orkney. Sutherland was the mainland *south* of the Orkney jarldom.

INDEX

Numbers in italics refer to the plates, roman numerals to colour plates